MEMOIRS OF A
REGULAR GUY

by
RJ Davenport III

Writers Club Press
San Jose · New York · Lincoln · Shanghai

Published by Writers Club Press, an imprint of iUniverse.com, Inc.

For information address:
iUniverse.com, Inc.
620 North 48th Street
Suite 201
Lincoln, NE 68504-3467
www.iuniverse.com

URL: http://www.writersclub.com

Dedication

This book is dedicated to my father who ignored me when I needed someone. He gave nothing, and I became something.

The earliest memories I can recall would start at about my teenage years…these may not be the earliest memories, but they are the ones I consider to be the most significant…

It started at about twelve, we…that is my family, and I were living in a section of Philadelphia called Germantown it was a black community but a nice little block. About 5 of us were cramped into a crappy two bedroom apartment. It was me, my brother, mother, sister, and mom's drunken boyfriend who we called Mr. Curtis. My sister slept in the living room we converted it into a bedroom for her use. Don't get confused by the term converted, when you're white, and have money converted means that you actually do remodeling, when you're black, it means that you put a bed into a room and BOOM! It's now converted into a bedroom.

We were all cramped into this tiny living space, but overall you can say we were happy, because we were together. It was at this time that my coming of age began…

I didn't get along very well with my sister we were constantly at each other's throat. There was however, an occasional time when we could have a laugh or two but these times were very few and far between.

I can remember plenty of times when I would be "exploring" around the house late at night and I would catch my sister masturbating in her bed. I got a kick out of catching her nothing sexual; I just found it funny to see her fingering herself, and making funny noises. Eventhough I had never had a woman, or jacked myself off I knew all too well from schoolyard talk and porno flicks what she was doing. Sometimes she would go at it like a madman! She would lay spread eagle on the bed under the covers. Her hand would be placed directly in her crotch area; she would be jackhammering away into herself. I would chuckle and laugh to myself everytime I saw this. No matter how many times I would catch her, it was always funny…Other than fight, and live together my sister and I didn't have much interaction at all…

I had a lot of friends around the neighborhood, and I would spend all my time outside into some neighborhood adventure. This was back in the day, when kids actually played outside instead of nowadays when they are killing each other.

When I first moved on this block I was sort of known right away. My brother introduced me to the most popular guy on the block…Merrill

Merrill and my brother went to high school together and it just so happened that he lived on the same block that we moved to. I thought Merrill was the funniest guy in the world! He was always cracking jokes and busting on people. Hanging with Merrill was like having your own private Eddie Murphy; he was just that funny. Eventhough Merrill and my brother were in high school, we all played together, not just us but all the kids played together. We played all the cool games football, manhunt, catch a girl freak a girl and we had fun! Big fun, the kind of fun times that kids today don't know anything about. Anyway knowing Merrill was as good as being in and he introduced me to everyone on the block.

On my first day moving in, I found myself in the middle of the street engaged in an intense game of football. I would hate to sound pretentious, but I was considered to be one of, if not the best in the neighborhood. I could out maneuver, stick, and catch the ball better than any person in my age group. I was even known for quite frequently making the older kids look stupid by catching a long touchdown pass while they had the unenviable job of covering me. I got quite a bit of notoriety for being a good football player. I was a legend! An actual street football hero. I have always regretted not going out for organized football in high school, or college. I think I had a special talent and I let it goto waste…

Times were different back then, as far as violence goes, that doesn't mean that we didn't have our rifts on the block. I remember each fight throughout my entire life as if it were yesterday. I don't know why but I just seem to clearly remember each altercation, in vivid detail....

My first involvement in fisticuffs came much earlier than the time period I'm describing now. I will make a break from the current storyline, and think back to about the 5th grade...I was a student at the Bannah school in West Philly, there was a classroom bully named Donnell.

Donnell used to hit, and smack the shit out of all the kids in the class CONSTANTLY. My head had a constant sting from the whacking the back of it would take. This was when hustler haircuts were in style, so if you know what a hustler haircut was then you know why my head had no padding, and would sting like a motherfucker when this guy would crack me one. So one day, I grew extremely tired of this daily torture. I stupidly challenged him to a fight after school in the park!

The remainder of the day I was scared shitless. I had never had a fight in my life, and here I was shooting off my big mouth about fighting after school. I should have just took the head slaps and lived to see another day. The minutes seemed to whiz by that day! Any other day in school, minutes seem like hours but today school seemed to end in 5 minutes. It was now three o'clock and my date with destiny was here!

The fight was scheduled to be in the park. Not just any park, but the park that just about the entire school walked home through! I wasn't thinking when I did this! The park was off school grounds so school officials couldn't save me. As I was walking to the park, all the kids in my class were hyping me up telling me *"YEAH, man you can do this! Kick this dude's ass!"* I was scared as hell, I mean it seemed like the whole school knew about this and they all showed up! It felt like the crowd was carrying me to the park. My legs were so wobbly from fear I could hardly walk. Finally, we made it to the park I didn't see Donnell. I looked around, but I didn't see him, I started to breathe a huge sigh of relief. Just as I was about to say "I guess he's not going to show up! Let's go home" here comes this guys strolling up...UHOH!

What happened next I don't even know if you could call it a fight. I was scared stiff, but figured I had one chance, so I lunged at him arms flailing wildly. Well he side stepped my pitiful attempt, and punched me in the mouth! My lip was busted, and I started to cry...fight over! I lost...with my busted lip, and pride I went home.

It was my last defeat ever...I guess that was good for me to get a taste of defeat, because since then I vowed to never let anyone kick my ass again. That decree still holds true to this day.

Back on the block, I was immediately sized up. There was already one champion in my age group...Reed.

Reed was a little younger than we were, but he was a big guy and he wasn't scared of anyone. He proved it on many occasions by knocking out all the dudes he fought. This made him the champ, and nobody messed with the champ. The guys didn't walk on eggshells around him, he would get kidded around with just like we all would but, only too a point. In the back of their minds they all knew if it went too far there would be hell to pay.

Reed and I were the biggest kids in the group so it was always known that if he and I ever mixed it up it would be something everybody would want to see. The battle eventually did take place after all, you can't have two kings in one court but we will get into that later...

My school life was not nearly as exciting as my home life, at least not now. In school I had friends, but not anything like the bonds I made on the block. I mostly succeeded with girls outside school at this point not that I had much success at all I mean I knew girls but I didn't really do much with them. I was mostly a talker when it came to girls, that means I was a liar and in retrospect I don't think I was alone.

I was in 7th grade and we were concerned with the normal things at that age new music, video games who had the hottest porno mags and of course...GIRLS.

There was a group of us that hung out in school it was Craig, Ali, Kevin, and me. There were other guys who would hang with us but this was the core group. We would eat lunch together, play or just hang out, Yes I did say play, Usually it was a game of 'CHINK' or good old 'Wall ball'. sometimes we could just hang out and talk about each others moms, but whatever we did we had a good time doing it.

I had my first girlfriend in seventh grade her name was Mikala.

Mikala was fine, she was in the 8th grade light skin...really light bright almost white and she had the biggest set of tits in the school, she was stacked!

Mikala and me were official boyfriend and girlfriend. She would wear my name belt all around school so everyone knew that she was "MY" girl. Eventhough she was my girl, she and Craig were very close, suspiciously close…

Craig was one of those sentimental, emotional, caring guys…you know the all around Boy Scout. The kind of guy women dream of but never get. I was a fun-loving, good time guy that cared about nobody's feelings but my own You know the kind of guy that always gets the girl. Despite the fact that she and Craig were so close I don't think she ever cheated on me with him.

I was sort of jealous of their relationship. Craig seemed closer to my girl than I was! These two would talk on the phone together for hours. I didn't' know if this was because she really dug him, or the fact that I didn't have a phone. Either way I didn't like it, but I guess she had to talk to somebody.

Mikala and I were just normal awkward 1st boyfriend and girlfriend. Other than the occasional arm around the waist we didn't have much physical contact. I think I only kissed her once or twice, but at least I had a girl, my first one and an older woman to boot.

For the duration of the relationship between the 2 of us, which lasted a full 2 months, which equals a decade at that age. Mikala and I ate lunch, walked home, and passed notes together…. Maybe not together but threegether! CRAIG was always there! Always in the middle! Always up in the business! Whenever I was walking with Mikala, Craig was always either there or on his way there. Hey, maybe she had two boyfriends, me as the fun one and Craig as the serious one.

Mikala and I broke up mid way through the school year, and I pretty much didn't care. We didn't hate each other after the breakup, it was just one of those things that happened. We still spoke to each other in passing and even held a brief conversation once or twice. It's been the most civil breakup I have ever had with a female.

However, not so strange Craig and Mikala still remained best of friends? I didn't expect him to stop talking to her because we fell out, but how about a little loyalty. I was curious about their relationship I questioned Craig about it and he assured me that everything was platonic...and I believed him? Little did I know that the summer would bring some interesting news from the two of them.

Besides a girlfriend, 7th grade only contained one other notable event for me and that was the losing of my virginity?

Diane was another 8th grader (what can I say I like em older) and she was my first Menage a trois!

Diane always liked me even when I was going with Mikala, but Diane was an original Ruff Ryder girl! She was cute, but using the words TOMBOY to describe her was an understatement. Diane was a fighter; always beating up girls...and boys and with Mikala out of the way I guess she figured I was hers for the taking...

Diane loved to play boys chase the girls. This was a fun game because you got to chase girls around the schoolyard, and freak them when you caught them. Guys always love free feels on girls. Diane wanted to go with me but she was too much of a TOMBOY for me. Back then, you didn't approach guys or a girl directly; you usually had a mediator. Of all people, my mediator was MIKALA! I don't know how it happened, but here I was sending diplomatic refusals to a new girl through my old girl! I could tell Diane was upset by me turning her down, but what can I say I have a reputation to protect. Eventhough I turned her down Diane wasn't finished with me yet...

One day in art class, that was the last class of the day. I was chilling with my buddy Mac. We were just making pictures, and Diane strolls up and informs us (in a letter of course the standard method of communication back then) that she had taken these pills earlier in the day that make her horny! The letter was addressed to me, but included Mac. She went on to state that not only was she horny, she was VERY HORNY! She was horny and wanted to fuck...both of us!

Needless to say I almost fell out of my chair. I mean can you believe it, here I am a 12 year old virgin and I thought *"HOLY SHIT!* I'm about to be involved in a threesome!" This was like a plot from a porno movie or something.

This note had me nervous but I had to play the cool role. Mac who was no virgin immediately accepted the invitation and I sheepishly accepted, mostly because he did. I had an image to uphold and I couldn't let these two non-virgins know that I was a virgin, scared, and without a clue of what I was about to do!

After it was established that everyone was up for it the next step was to find a place. Lucky me, I was the only one who had a place that no one was at home during the day or so I thought. After school the plan was to goto my house for a good old after school threesome, needless to say the news of the impending afternoon shenanigans spread like wildfire. Everyone was coming up to us to ask if it was true. We were like superstars; I knew that if this came off correctly, the next day our popularity would burst through the stratosphere! I tried to keep cool answering everyone's questions, faking it like I was about to give her the fucking of her life! Behind the scenes I was practically shitting my pants...I mean what the hell was I going to do? I have NO idea of how to fuck properly and on top of that I have to bang her in front of someone else! I certainly got myself into another jacked up situation. It was now three o'clock and another after school day of reckoning had arrived...Everyone saw the three of us leaving together on the LONG WALK HOME. Now that everyone saw us leave together, even if I chickened out, I knew that there would be no disputing the story when we came to school tomorrow. Everybody knew what we were going to do!

That afternoon was a long walk, I felt like I was going to the electric chair! I kept feeling like I was about to throw up! I kept up a good front though, and neither of them knew that I really didn't want to do this. Conversation flowed normal, although I was a little quiet. I kept thinking I was going to faint as we drew closer and closer to my house.

After what seemed like hours we finally made it there and guess what? Mr. Curtis was home! What the fuck? As I put the key in the door and slowly opened it, I heard his GODDAMNED slippers sliding across the floor, as he made his way around the house. I was like damn, I can't believe this fucker was here! This should have been my way out, I don't know why, but I started thinking of ways that we could still pull this off! I guess I got a little courage because I wasn't going to let Mr. Curtis stop me! I closed the door back took a second and then it came to me…**the basement!**

The apartment we lived in was a big house converted into apartments, so access to the basement was outside. The door was never locked, and the basement wasn't finished it was dark and musty, not your typical fucking environment, but today it was going to do fine! So around the back of the house we all went.

There was a little light in the darkened area and I quickly turned it on, once we were inside. Mac and I laid our coats on the floor as a little makeshift bed, and just like an old pro Diane was naked in seconds! Now my nervousness returned, Mac was quick to say, *"I'm going first!"* he got no argument from me! I was like *"sure go ahead knock yourself out"*. I mean, I was scared as all hell, I wasn't about to argue about who got sloppy seconds.

Mac pulled his pants down and started doing her while I sucked her tits and kissed her. This guy's face was inches away from mine, breathing all hard as he pumped away at her teenage pussy. In the back of my mind I was thinking *"HOLY SHIT!" I'm gonna have to do that in a minute!* In addition to the pressure of this being my first time, Mac being there, and the fact that we were in a fucking basement that Goddamned Mr. Curtis kept walking around every 2 seconds. I could here his stupid slippers scraping across the floor. There were back steps that led out of the apartment and came down directly in front of the basement door. I was hoping this jack off wasn't about to come downstairs for some stupid reason. This would have been a very embarrassing situation to be caught in especially by him!

I'm trying my best to relax while kissing this girl, while Mac humped away blowing his hot ass breath in my ear. Just as I start to relax a little, there he goes again with his slippers back and forth. The fucker would hardly move when everyone was home, but now he is upstairs moving around like he is in a cardio-funk class. I swear I even heard the back door open once.

After what seemed like an eternity, Mac gets up and says, *"ok you're up buddy!"* I think to myself, *"Gee thanks!"* I think my heart stopped, I reluctantly switched positions. I don't think Mac came I think he just got tired, but nevertheless it was my turn at bat…do I hit a homerun or strike out?

Mac started up where I left off, kissing and sucking Diane. This guy didn't waste any time, I thought he was in total control. Mac never missed a beat; he was smooth like I was supposed to be!

I attempted to prepare for the task at hand. I pulled my pants down and I was so scared that I couldn't "rise to the occasion" if you get my meaning, and if you don't **'I COULDN'T GET A HARD ON!"**

I stroked my dick, thought of every sexy thought I could imagine, but my dick just would not cooperate! I even rubbed my dick on her pussy, but still nothing I was too scared to get hard so I faked it! I stuck my finger in her pussy and went for broke. She seemed to enjoy it but I couldn't tell if she knew the difference.

After what I determined to be an appropriate amount of time I stopped, and the festivities were over.

I breathed a sigh of relief and sent Mac and Diane on their way. Eventhough, I didn't do anything I felt like a hero after it was over. I was like, *"HMMM, I have been to the mountaintop"*.

The next day in school we were superstars! Everyone knew and in each class we were being interviewed like we discovered plutonium. Diane even wanted to do it again, but I said, **"NO!** *I wasn't into it"*. I was playing it off to the fellas like she was no good, but thinking in my mind that there was no way I was doing that again, I was too scared! Oh, how times have changed for me!

With that incident passed the 7th grade was over. Diane and Mikala would be graduating and off to high school. Diane's going to Germantown and Mikala is going to Saul high school. I managed to pass all of my classes and in the fall I would be a big time 8th grader running shit! It's the summer now and time to hang out.

Summertime on the block revolved around playing sports, hanging out, and ranking on each others mom sometimes the older guys would tell us crazy stories about themselves having sex…probably lies. Since I was technically still a virgin, I was very interested in these stories. I was hoping I could learn something so that next time I would be more prepared. I had watched plenty of porno and had an endless supply of hardcore mags, but I still lacked real life experience.

One day I was sitting in my room alone I can't recall where all the household members were but I was the only one home. I lived 2 doors away from Vince; he was one of my buddies from the block. Vince's house was packed. It seemed like every family member he had lived in the house with him, one member I remember vividly was his Aunt Crystal…

Crystal was a loose whore, she was about 26 had a nice ass with a huge gap, and a perfect set of tits and she would always come out braless with a tanktop. I would always stare at her because you could clearly see her nipples through her shirt; this would always send me through the roof! I would get so crazed over her; I would look as much as possible. Secretly, I wanted to fuck the shit out of her, but I never said anything to anyone about it, the fellas would have talked about me like crazy.

Everybody knew Crystal was a no good Whore, and they would always dog her out. I secretly wanted to fuck her…**BADLY!** I wonder if they did too? She was a bar whore, always in a bar and fucking someone from it. We would all rank on her and there wasn't anything Vince could do because all of us would talk about her.

So like I said one day I was home alone and I looked out the window and saw her in the backyard hanging up clothes. Crystal was clearly visible in her yellow tanktop **(NO BRA),** and blue jean shorts. I was cursing myself for not having a pair of binoculars! Luckily, I didn't' need them to see those huge nipples poking out of her shirt. Crystal must have been constantly horny, or cold, because her nipples always looked like they had just been iced down, and today they were more pronounced than ever! While watching her I noticed that I got a tremendous hard on. I don't know where the idea came from but I stripped off all of my clothes!

While I was undressing, I never took my eyes off Crystal. Once I was totally naked my hand found it's way to my dick, and I began to stroke it while looking at her hang up these clothes. I had never done this before but it felt too good to stop! I was scooping her entire body from head to toe, all the while pumping my dick faster and faster!

A bottle of Cocoa butter caught my eye, and I put two and two together and before you know it here I am watching Vince's aunt hang up clothes, while stroking my lotion covered dick!

After a while, she finished with the clothes and went in the house, but I was just beginning...

I laid on the bed and pumped like there was no tomorrow!

All of a sudden this incredible feeling of shockwaves went through my entire body and stopped at my dick. It began to feel all tingly and I shot out this mysterious goo. I wasn't sure what happened, all I knew was that what ever just happened I was hooked on it! From that point on, I was jerking off on a regular basis with every lubricant you can imagine. If it smeared it went on my dick. No picture of a scantily clad woman was safe in the house. I would jack off to essence magazine, the Spiegel catalog, and of course my favorite Victoria's secret. I loved to shoot cum all over these gorgeous women! My all-time favorite was the jet beauty of the week.

We used to get a subscription to Jet, and I would always tear out the jet beauty. I was covering a new babe every week with my jism!

I never got caught jerking, but I had a couple of close calls.

I remember one night I was whacking it to one of my favorite jet beauties. Of all places to jack my dick in the house I chose the kitchen. I had just greased up my dick with some used cooking oil, laid on the floor by the stove and I was going to town. I was just about to shoot when I hear my mother coming down the hallway! I thought… *"OH SHIT!"*

Who wants to be caught by their mom jerking off! I got up and tried to walk calmly to my room. If I would have ran it would have caused too much suspicion. I walked quickly, but I was also at the point of no return with my jerking so while walking I'm shooting cum all over my shorts and down my leg!

As I entered my room, out of the corner of my eye I saw my mom enter the kitchen. I don't know if she could tell I was nude with a big cum covered dick. If she did know she never said anything, and I wasn't asking!

My closest friend on the block was Raymond. Ray was Merrill's brother; he and I were pretty much alike. Our birthdays are 1-day apart, maybe that's why we were such good friends. We would always hang out together. we would sneak out late at night and play monopoly together for hours. Mostly it was him sneaking; my mother was pretty lenient as long as she knew where I was going she gave me the freedom to go.

Ray's mom was a little more strict, and very embarrassing. Not just because she weighed about 400 pounds, but because she would stand in the middle of the street and yell at the top of her lungs **MERRILL! RAYMOND! LET'S GO!**

Everyday when it was time for them to come in, no matter where you were in the neighborhood you could hear her giant bellow throughout the entire block. When she spouted off it was like a foghorn, and they would go running up the block to get home, we would all die laughing!

Their mother provided a never-ending source of material for us to make fun of them about. The joking always ended in the same way with someone doing a sidesplitting rendition of their mother summoning them home.

They were always called home to do some stupid task, like change a channel or get a cup of juice. can you imagine being called all the way home from down the block just to get your mom a cup of juice? She would be sitting in the kitchen, and bellow for one of them to come home.

Boy her fat ass sure did have a good set of pipes. We could hear her around the corner. I didn't like her much but she wasn't' my mother (what a relief).

It was ironic that my closest friend on the block would be my first test in the neighborhood.

Best friends have their problems with each other. Ray was thought of as second toughest behind Reed. I had no ranking since I had no fights, but that was about to change…

One day Ray kept annoying the hell out of me. It was during these days that my temper was as quick as a hair trigger. This guy kept fucking with me no matter how many times I told him to quit it! Finally I was ready to break his jaw, but Ray didn't want to fight. Maybe he was a little intimidated, but I was thoroughly annoyed and would not be denied handing out this ass whipping which he kept asking for!

Just as we started to circle each other, and get the fight on…the foghorn sounded (lucky for him). we could see the huge girth of his mother bellowing in the middle of the street for him to come home…

It was late in the day when this altercation happened and even after a night of sleep I was still livid.

The next day my brother and I walked up to Ray's house. When we got to his house Ray just happened to be at the window, and I called him out to fight

He wouldn't come out of the house. Merrill came out and said, *"My brother should stop acting like a punk and fight!"*

Merrill didn't dislike his brother, but he knew the code of the street and when beef was had it needed to be settled! Finally after several minutes of ridicule, Ray came out.

I thought he came out to fight, but I think he wanted to eat me because he had forks and knives all over his body. They were in his pockets, socks even in the waistband of his pants! I though Damn I must evoke some type of fear in people. After his brother stripped him of the weapons the fight was on!

It lasted about 30 seconds, with me punching Ray in the eye and him running into the house. It wasn't satisfying but I took the victory, however this would not be the only time he and I would lockhorns. Ray would be given another chance for revenge.

One particularly embarrassing moment in the summer came with the event, which became known as the RJ-RJ girls. I was teased the whole summer about my lack of response to this situation.

One night we were all on the front porch playing Monopoly. All of a sudden out of the blue somebody on the porch said, *"RJ, somebody is calling you"*. I said, *"shut up!"* and kept on playing. Then he said it again and this time I heard it too…

Faintly in the distance I could hear a group of female chanting my name over, and over *'RJ, RJ, RJ!'* It kept getting louder, and louder and closer, and closer.

Finally the chant was right next to us. I looked off the porch to the right of me, and there they were three of the neighborhood girls Gerri, Shonda, Tina.

They were in the middle of the street chanting my name as they walked by. Shonda even stopped and simulated riding a guy while screaming my name in ecstasy!

I was dumbfounded, these three hot girls whom I hardly even ever spoke to were chanting for me! I didn't know what to do everyone was stunned, but the shock quickly wore off and the advice came. *"Man you better go get those girls!" "You better hurry up and go ahead man!" "Stop being a pussy and go fuck them!"*

These statements were coming at me from all angles; I had no idea of how to handle this situation. I had tried a threesome once with disastrous results, and now here was 3 girls wanting to do me!

So, I did the obvious thing. I played it off, and continued with the game. This was not a popular decision. I was teased for weeks especially after Merrill went up to Tina (one of the RJ-RJ girls), and asked her why they did it her response still shocks me to this day.

She said, *"our parents weren't home, and we wanted him to come over and get with us"*. I could have fucking died! This was some porno type shit; a dream come true and I blew it AGAIN! I never lived that moment down I don't regret not going, but I do wonder what it would have been like.

With the summer in full swing, and the temperature rising so will some tempers. It seemed mine was always at the boiling point. My next challenge could have turned into a serious matter had the whole block not come to save this kid neck...

One afternoon we were all hanging around outside. One of my buddies, Mike made some remark to me that set me off.

Mike was a trash talker who was never willing to backup his words. His most notable act was being beaten up so badly by Reed, that he suffered an asthma attack in the middle of the street. His mother had to be called to the scene to attend to her pussy of a son. How embarrassing it is not to only get your ass kicked, and then to have your mother come and pick your beaten ass out of the middle of the street. I have to give it to Reed that was a classic knockout that went down in the street fight history!

I knew Mike was a pussy, but he went to far and had to defend himself.

He was talking shit, and I called him out on it in front of everybody. Even if you are a total bitch if you hope to get any respect at all if someone calls you out you better go!

I said to him, "What's up pussy?" if you are going to keep talking shit put your mother fucking hands up bitch!

Then advanced on him. I could see the look of fear in his eyes, and I knew I had him. At that point Mike did something that shocked the hell out of me…he ran.

Mike looked me directly in the eye, turned and raced back to his house like he had a rocket up his ass. I was angry, but I wasn't about to chase him. I would see him again and we could settle up at that time. Everyone thought the same thing that I did…Pussy!

Mark stayed in the house until later that night…

I was off on some other adventure at Ray's house, and had put the incident out of my mind. It was about 8 p.m. I didn't know this but Mike had come back outside and was at the bottom of the block getting his heart pumped up by the people down there. They told him that he shouldn't go out like a punk, he should go and **kick my ass!**

He must have believed what they said, because when Ray and me were heading down the block he met me halfway followed by a crowd of people and said, *"you want to fight me?"*

I thought, "oh this boy is finally getting some heart". My response was, "let's do this"…

We walked to the middle of the street. Everybody was out on their porches, and lined the sidewalk for some reason a prime time event! As soon as we reached the street, Mike whipped off his name belt to use as a weapon! I said *"hold up"*.

I went directly in my house and began a frantic search for my name belt. If he wanted to play rough I was down. Well the ruckus

I caused looking for my belt alerted my mother and brother that there was trouble brewing.

Mom came in my room where I was frantically throwing things around, and wanted to know what was going on. I didn't respond I just continued my search, and she continued questioning. I was growing angrier by the minute because I couldn't find my goddamn belt! Finally I gave up looking for it; I was just going to fight without a weapon. I rushed for the door with my brother right on my heels followed my mother.

Just as I was about to exit the house I saw something in the corner that I would have loved to use on that punk...my bat!

I grabbed the bat and raced out the door. I figured if this faggot wanted to play dirty so was I! My mother was right behind me, but she wasn't fast enough. By the time she got to the porch I was already in the street.

What seemed like a million people were gathered out there now. I raced at Mike with my bat raised high. Mike cringed in fear. what a bitch he was! I didn't get far; Merrill was the first to grab me.

He couldn't hold me alone; I was determined to get at Mike. I was just about to break free of Merrill's grip when someone else grabbed me! Everyone was now trying to restrain me from killing this kid.

It took a whole group of people to stop me. I don't know who was grabbing me because there were so many hands reaching for me. I was hell-bent on busting this guy's ass, and I guess they saw this because they did everything they could to stop me. During this entire ruckus Mike retreated to his house again. Everyone must have thought I was crazy, I think they knew they had just saved that guy's ass.

Mike didn't come out the next day, but he did the following day. We were outside playing ball; Mike came and joined in. Back then grudges didn't go for long and all was forgiven, but I didn't forget. I never looked at Mike any other way than as a total bitch after that day.

I can respect a man for fighting and losing, but not running.

One of the next classic moments from that summer have to rank up in the top ten of all time stupid things that I have ever done. I can't believe I'm putting this in here but here goes...

We lived next door to a house full of lesbians, and homos. The two main ones that I knew by name were Tim (the gay guy), and Audrey (the lesbian). They were always entertaining gay friends in their home, and there were so many fags in and out of there that I couldn't keep up with the names. Anyway I was a horny kid and Audrey wasn't' much to look at, but she had a nice set of tits. I was an admirer of hers, but of course I kept this a secret kept this info locked away with my lust for crystal. If it ever got out that I looked at Audrey in that way I would have been a laughing stock.

The homo house had a deck built onto it that was parallel with the window in my bedroom. Audrey used to eat noodles out there everyday while reading the paper. If I looked out of my room window I could clearly see her, but I was careful so she wouldn't see me. I would spend a lot of time stroking my dick watching her tits as she sat eating her goddamn noodles. I must have been pretty horny, because she wasn't even wearing anything sexy but I would still stroke my dick.

One day, I got the idea and wrote her a note. I wrapped the note around a rock, and threw it up on the deck while they weren't home. I watched and waited for her to get home and hopefully be the 1st to find and read the letter. This is what it said:

Dear Audrey,

You don't know me, but I live close to your house. When you come outside it gets me so hot to watch you. Please come out more often with as little on as possible.

Signed,

Your secret admirer

Atleast I wasn't stupid enough to sign my name. I was so excited wondering what she would do when she saw it. When she got home she went out on the deck like clockwork, and saw the note. She picked it up, and went in the house.

I watched that deck from my window, and waited. Then she came outside!

The only problem was she was dressed in her same frumpy old outfit, but she was out there and she knew she was being watched.

I decided to get bold. I stripped down to nothing, stood up on the windowsill and stuck my rock hard dick through the curtains.

I don't' know if she saw me or not, but this went on for 2 days. I grew tired of getting my dick hard, shoving it through the curtain, and having it bake in the sun without getting any gratification. So, I gave up.

I moved on to other things, but I still would sneak a peek at Audrey every now and then when she would use her deck.

Ray's try at revenge came on a rainy day when my brother and me were at his house just hanging out. Ray was being a dickhead he kept taking these stupid ass GI Joe figures that he collected and putting it in my face. He was annoying the hell out of me! Finally I got tired of it and told him, ***"stop it! or I I'm going to kick your ass!"***.

Ray put the man down and said, ***"Fuck you!"*** I thought, *"ok its time for round 2"*.

We postured in front of each other to see who would throw the first punch. All this is going on in Merrill's living room! Merrill & my brother were sitting on the couch. Again, it's not that they didn't care but they understood the code of the streets. So a fair fight was on!

After circling each other Ray pushed me, I responded with a shot to the left eye that sent him tumbling to the floor, he never recovered. He just laid there for about 5 minutes, got up and went upstairs. he didn't' come back. We all had a laugh after he left, it's a shame it had to happen in his own house, but he deserved it.

The winner and still champion!

Startling event over the summer...My mother and Mr. Curtis break up!

I was never too fond of Mr. Curtis. I was never too fond of any of my mother's choices for men. They have all been **losers! BIG TIME LOSERS!**

She seemed to always pick someone who had a problem. Mr. Curtis's problem was he was a boozer.

This guy would drink morning, afternoon, and night. He was never abusive to us, but his drinking was causing obvious problems. The two of them would get into violent arguments all the time. I was scared sometimes, because I was just a kid. If this drunkard finally flipped the fuck out how could I defend the family?

One day my mother finally got bold, and put him out!

At last peace was restored to the house, but would it last?

While I was away for one of my nightmare weekend visits with my father, Mr. Curtis came back. He didn't come back to live but to destroy!

He kicked the door in, and ransacked the house. My mother informed me over the telephone. She told me that I would be staying at my father's house until she could get the house back in order.

I protested, not only because I wanted to come home to see if everything was ok, but I didn't' want to stay at my father's indefinitely. Not only was my request denied, but I was told my brother would be shipped to my Dad's as well.

What a bummer my father and brother under the same roof! This was supposed to be vacation! The next few weeks with my father and brother were awful. Each day we would wake up, or should I say be awakened at 8 a.m. We had to shower, eat, and get out.

We would be forced to stay outside like it was a job. Our shift was from 9 to 8 with a lunch break at 12.

This routine went on for 3 weeks. While we were outside my pop would be in the house fucking one of his flavors of the month. One day I couldn't stand it any longer. I was sick of sitting in the park all day. I went back in the house I was greeted with a frowning, *'What are you doing in here?'*. I said, *" I'm tired of being outside, and I'm coming in!"*. Minutes later I was right back outside. I was told to go back out, or I would be wishing I could **SIT** in the park.

Finally our sentence was reprieved; my mother called and told us we could come home. I was thoroughly sick of my dad, and brother. I was ready to leave now! In a little while I would be back on the block where I felt comfortable.

The return home felt kind of strange at first, but soon I was back in the swing of things. News of what happened traveled quickly through the block, and our disappearance was questioned. Everybody was cool about it, which made the situation easier to deal with.

I was surprised there was no ribbing about it. if there was ever a time the crew showed sympathy, I guess this was one of them.

With the summer now drawing to a close Labor Day was upon us. Everyone was getting the same disease the ' *Go back to school blues'*; and I had a bad case of it. The summer was a good time of hanging out, and playing and I didn't want it to end.

It was an unusually hot day during the last days of vacation. We were all at the playground playing basketball. Reed, and I were watching on the side since it was mostly the older guys were playing. I was horsing around by a tree when Reed threw a rock at me I guess to get my attention. He didn't hit me, but he came close enough.

I shrugged it off, but he kept doing it. With each throw he was getting closer, and closer. Finally, I told the guy to cut it the fuck out! This jackass didn't' listen, and kept on doing it! I thought to myself this is finally it, the battle is about to happen!

I stepped to Reed, and he didn't back down. He was right back in my face wolfing at me the same way I was wolfing at him. The basketball game stopped, and everyone watched, they knew something was about to happen.

Reed's brother was among some of the guys that were playing ball. He immediately began screaming for Reed to kick my ass! His brother always thought his little brother was the greatest fighter in the world, but I was about to show him otherwise...

My brother was also there, he was trying to break it up, but the old-heads and Reed's brother convinced him to let us settle it like men. I decided the time for talk was over. I started the action by punching him dead in the fucking eye! Reed stumbled, but didn't drop. He then swung back, but missed. I thought this guy was incredibly slow, and I knew instantly that this was going to be a cakewalk.

I hit Reed again, with a solid shot to the jaw. Then I followed with another, and another. now this guy finally hit the ground....

Hard! He didn't get in one punch! I was surprised at how slow he was! Every punch this guy threw I could see coming a mile away. After I had him on the ground I proceeded to finish him off!

When I was done, Reed was bleeding from the mouth and nose, then the guys stepped in and stopped the fight.

Now Reed's brother was livid! I thought he wanted to take over for his beaten brother, and try to fight me! He was screaming at the top of his lungs, **"IT'S NOT OVER!"**. He kept repeating this numerous times, but from the way Reed lay sprawled out on the ground, I could tell…it was over!

My brother kept trying to convince this guy to let it go the matter had been settled. Reed's brother was incensed, and wouldn't drop the issue. meanwhile Reed had begun to drag himself to his feet. He sat on a log, and you could tell he was in no shape or mood to try to fuck with me again.

The fight was over! I went home to keep Reed's brother and my brother from getting into it. Before I left I looked at Reed to see if he wanted more, but he just sat slumped over on a log looking pitiful.

I went back to the block.

The news spread quickly of what happened. I was now the block champ. I was about to be in 8th grade, and I had a huge chip on my shoulder and dared anyone to try to knock it off!

The first day of school, and OH, how I was dreading it! Once I walked through those big green doors, the smell of school hallway hit me. I saw my old friends walking down the hall, and I forgot all about the pain of being in school.

We all got together and began talking about our summer vacations. One thing we were all glad about is that we were all 8th graders and we ruled the school!

During recess, Craig and me hooked up in the yard. Everyone else was playing ball. We were alone, and I guess he felt this was the appropriate moment and he hit me with some news.

He said, "I talked to Mikala over the summer". I tried to keep cool, and nonchalantly asked him, "what did she have to say?"

I hadn't talked to, or seen Mikala since she graduated last year. I stopped by her house over the summer once, but she wasn't home. I had forgotten all about her, but I wanted to if she had asked about me.

Craig said he and Mikala had had numerous phone conversations over the summer. She told him she was going through some rough times with her mother, and needed a friend to talk about it with. Mikala's mom was strict, and overbearing. She would punish Mikala severely for minor behavioral infractions. He told me that Mikala had run away a couple of times, and a lot of this was going on while me and her were still involved. She made him promise not to tell....

Why didn't that bitch tell me? I was her man, and she was confiding in this prick. I felt cheated; I didn't let my displeasure with the situation show. I just let him keep talking to see where the story was leading. I wasn't prepared for the bombshell that was dropped next.

Craig told me about a time over the summer when she ran away and showed up at his house at 1 a.m. Now in my mind I'm freaking out, because I have a feeling I know what's coming next. I never knew if Mikala was a virgin, but I knew Craig had fucked before. Anyway, she appears on his doorstep in the late night hour. She was crying about some stupid problem with her mother. Craig being the gentleman invites her in to sleep on the couch for the rest of the night.

Now I'm seething, and waiting for him to deliver the dagger through the heart and tell me the rest. He continues, and says he gave her some clothes to change into and she starts crying and blah, blah, blah. the next thing you know they start kissing…. **WHAT THE FUCK?** Then they start heavy petting, touching, feeling, **TIT SUCKING**.

Finally the ultimate insult…he banged her!

Right there on the goddamn couch. He screwed my girl! That bastard…. He was a lucky bastard! I couldn't believe it, I wasn't mad because I still liked Mikala. I was mad because I put in the work of going with her and he reaped all the benefits. I began to 3rd degree him about her wonderful melons, but Craig wouldn't divulge the info. Giving explicit details wasn't his style he would say, "*a gentleman never kisses and tells*"…what a **FAG!**

That was the last conversation we ever had about Mikala. I didn't' even want to hear about her anymore. No hard feelings though because there are plenty of women to go around!

8th grade came, and went like a whirlwind! I have to admit I was expecting a lot more, but it was pretty uneventful. There were no relationships, or major incidents. Oh, maybe just one…the breakup of my father and me!

My dad wasn't around that much. He would do the weekend dad thing, but it didn't' seem like he was doing it willingly.

My father was a cheap bastard! I can remember I would have to contribute from my allowance just to get a birthday present for myself. I thought he was a big dickhead! My dad always found every flaw in my appearance, and if there wasn't one he would make up one. If my hair wasn't combed to his specifications I was royally reamed, if my fingernails weren't properly cut I got trashed! It didn't matter to him who was around when he doled out his verbal assault either. If he met up with one of his friends I was always introduced as his hard head. I didn't have a name it was just, *"HI, Bob this is my hard head"*. I hated it! I don't know why, but I still wanted to be with him. Eventhough my weekends with him were HELL, It felt good when my father would come to pick me up.

The other kids didn't have a dad around, so it made me feel special when he would drive up in his big fancy Lincoln. His car would always be shinny, and clean, it would just glisten in the sunlight. Everybody would stare enviously as we drove off in luxury…

My smile would quickly change into a frown, because as soon as I got into the car his nonstop badgering would begin. One day I got in the car and I don't know where it came from but this is what happened…

I sat down, and he asked me, *"What is wrong with your hair?"*. I was told to get in the house, and comb it properly…NOW! He had this real disgusted look on his face. I was 12 years old for chrissake; do you expect me to look like I just stepped off of G.Q. magazine? I was tired of his constant criticisms; so I took a deep breath opened the car door and slammed it shut. I went in the house, and never looked back. I peeked out the window, and saw him drive off.

I could almost see the smoke coming out of his ears, and dissipating out of the sunroof of his shiny new Lincoln. I went to my room and sat down. Suddenly there was a knock at the front door. it wasn't a friendly knock but a harsh one. *Was he back?* I wondered, and if he was what was I going to do? I stood frozen in place for what seemed like hours, finally I went to the door and I asked through the double lock…. *Who is it?* As if I didn't know. He responded with a *sharp "OPEN THE DOOR!"*

I was frozen in my tracks; I didn't know what to do next. If I opened that door he would certainly have put his foot nice, and deep into my ass! By no means was I in the mood for a beating, so I went out the backdoor. I climbed over the fence, and went through the neighbor's yard onto the porch of one of my friends. From that safe distance I watched him exit the vestibule, get in his car and drive away. This time when he drove off I'm sure I saw flames coming out of that sunroof.

I breathed a sigh of relief when he was gone. I wasn't sad, I was glad I wasn't with him. I wondered what my mother would say when she got home…would she make me call him or would she support my decision? Her reaction surprised me. When I told her what happened, She laughed. I proclaimed that I was never going to call, or go to his house again! My mother just said, *"You are both too stubborn, and need to work it out .*" She has never really pushed me to do anything that I didn't want to do, and she said that she also told him the same thing. When my dad told her his version of the story he said, "*in order for him to have any contact with him I would have to call him, and let him kick my ass then after that we could be together again*"...IS HE CRAZY? What kid is going to make an appointment for a spanking? I wasn't about to do this, so I never called and neither did he. It's been 16 years since I've last talk to my father. I don't' see how you could abandon your own child for something so silly.

School was now rapidly drawing to a close, and graduation was near. For our graduation trip the class went to the Annapolis Naval base.

On a Friday afternoon in June we all climbed into a giant tour bus. I had never been on a bus like this before! To me this bus was like riding in a limo. The seats were velour with footrests, and they reclined! Can you believe it? I almost flipped when I noticed that the bus had a bathroom on it. WOW, this was living! I wasn't too crazy about going to Annapolis, but at-least we were going in style.

On any school trip usually the bus ride is the most exciting. That's where you play games and get into all kinds of fun. The teachers were choosing who could go on which bus, and I got stuck on the bus with every dufus who was in the eighth grade! Not one of my buddies or anybody interesting was on my bus. This trip was going to **SUCK!**

I was on the reject bus, and I was sitting next to the weirdest kid in the class. He would always talk to himself, and have these wild pretend fantasies about unicorns and shit like that. This was now a nightmare. After what seemed like an endless ride we finally got to Annapolis and no offense to the people that live there but Annapolis **SUCKS!**

This was not only my opinion, but it was the general consensus of the entire class. We were all sick of seeing stupid landmarks, and couldn't have been more bored looking at this dumb ass naval base. The only people who seemed to enjoy this navy base were the girls. they would flirt with every navy guy that they saw! As if these **MEN**, would be interested in talking to some schoolgirls. After nonstop sightseeing it was finally time to go home.

As we were about to board the bus for our return trip, I noticed some people switching busses. I saw my crew in the window of the other bus, and they motioned for me to get on. Needless to say I did! I couldn't stomach another 2 hours of that guy screaming to himself about trolls and unicorns.

This bus was all that! Every popular person was on this bus. They had all the ingredients of a successful ride a radio, food, and girls.

All the hottest girls were on this bus. Due to a lack of seating, I was lucky enough to have one of the finest females in the class planted firmly on my lap for the entire ride home, or should I say grind home. This girl was Veronica, we never spoke much and I'm surprised that she sat on my lap. Veronica had the biggest ass in the school, and every guy wanted to hit it. She had a boyfriend, but he wasn't on the trip.... Lucky for me.

Sitting next to us was Karen, since Mikala graduated Karen was now the holder of the biggest tits in the school title. Karen's face could scare a ghost, but she had an incredible rack. I has in heaven I had a girl on my lap to my side and all over and my boys in the back after a lot of joking talking and everyone checking my pants for a hard on we started up a game of the ever popular truth or dare.

I think horny guys made up this game just so they can kiss and feel girls. I got called on plenty of times, and I must have kissed every girl in my vicinity. The most memorable kiss was veronica.

Veronica and I must have kissed 5 or six times that night. Each kiss went longer, and longer sometimes we didn't even stop! I loved every minute of this. I was even enjoying kissing Karen, with her dogface. One time I was called on to kiss her I got kind of bold, and put my hand on one of those huge melons. Oh it felt so good! Her tit was soft, and I could barely fit my hand on it, she didn't even put up a fight. She let me explore her huge firm breasts without protest. I never wanted this ride to end, but before I knew it we were pulling up in the school parking lot. We all piled off the bus and said our good byes.

I rushed home and called (we had a phone now) my friends up to discuss the trip. These were conference calls; because I would call someone on the three-way then they would call someone and so on. we had a huge phone party.

We talked about this all weekend I was happy the entire weekend.

Monday was back to school only the party had stopped. News of the trip spread all throughout the school, and pretty soon it got back to you know who…veronica's boyfriend.

People hyped up the event. They were saying all kinds of things to him, like I was rock hard, and she was rubbing her ass all on my dick. Rumor spreaders are real assholes! Eventually this guy got fed up, and wanted to fight me. He approached me and started questioning me about the situation. Now I'm no punk, but I didn't want to fight this guy over a girl who obviously didn't care about him, and wasn't interested in me much either.

He never touched me; he just talked, and complained. I didn't let it escalate I just told him to take his problem up with his girl NOT ME! I guess he thought that was good advice because he took it and left me alone…

They broke up the next day. Nothing further ever developed with veronica, and me. We never even talked anymore after that, just an occasional hello. It doesn't matter to me because I had a ball on the bus.

Graduation day was not as exciting as I thought it would be. During practice I couldn't wait for the actual event, but when the day came I wasn't excited at all. Another thing that made it a bring down is that when I walked in my family wasn't there.

They didn't arrive until all the graduates were seated onstage. I guess they were on cp time that day. It was nice when they finally arrived. My mother 2 nieces and sister all came to see my biggest accomplishment. I felt like a king. I thought there would be something special after graduation was over like dinner or presents; but there was nothing. We just went home, money was tight in those days but I was still hoping for at least a dinner.

Graduation evening I just hung around outside. The original plans were to goto my brother's graduation, but that got scrapped due to the fact that he was not graduating. He had to goto summer school because he failed a class so much for his moment in the sun. In the fall it would be off to high school but for now it's summer again.

There was a growing friction between my brother and mother ever since he didn't graduate. One day they had a huge argument over something dumb and my brother just moved out without a word to anyone. he just left like a thief in the night.

With him gone I was now the man of the house. I welcomed my role as protector and king of my domain. I was getting more privileges, and this was the beginning of my spin out of control.

Summer had come and as the days of going to high school drew nearer I started getting more and more nervous. The older guys who were in high school already would fill all the new freshmen's heads with stories of the dreaded "Freshmen Day" and stuff about teachers and students being stabbed I didn't let it show but I was scared!

I was going to be a student at Lincoln high way out in the northeast, a white neighborhood. I was tortured with endless stories about how the Klan was going to get me, and that I would be in the middle of race wars these sound silly but I was nervous and now dreading the 1st day of school. We were also told that we were going to get our asses kicked daily just for being freshmen the way they were describing high school it didn't sound like a picnic

The day was finally here. Would I be the victim of violence? Would I escape without getting my ass kicked? I was about to find out.

I chose my wardrobe carefully that day. I had on my burgundy lee jeans; a black chams debarron shirt, and my black Todd 1 sweatsuit jacket. I was fly! I'll never forget the scene as the bus pulled up to the school.

People were everywhere, These guys were big, and scary looking. I was even more nervous now. The most surprising thing was that this school was deep in the northeast, which is a white area, and there were just as many blacks as there are whites.

I was shitting my pants as the bus pulled to a stop and we all had to get off. I could hardly believe the carnage that was going on. Junior high was nothing compared to how rowdy and loud these people were I felt totally out of place not to mention that everyone seemed to know somebody I looked like the only person who didn't know a soul. I was trying to look cool but I felt stupid walking up to this giant school alone. I stepped off the bus and looked across the street there was one long cement path that bisected the middle of a huge green field. this path led up to the front door of a building where I would soon have 4 great years of experience…Abraham Lincoln.

As I walked up the pathway, I was aghast at the size of the campus. It seemed more like college than high school. The giant front lawn was littered with bodies of relaxing students. Some were sitting while others stood. From the conversations I overheard they were all reminiscing over old times and summer vacation. I kept wondering how could they all know each other?

High School women are incredible! My mouth must have hung open all day as I stared at overly developed tits, and some of the nicest asses I have ever seen! The girls I had been with before were nothing compared to these WOMEN!

As I pass these girls I'm thinking these amazons must be seniors. But they were **freshmen!** They are going into the same classroom as me! How can such beauty be the same age as me? I began to daydream about scoring with one of these bitches, if I had to die trying I was going to score with one of them.

From the outside Lincoln looked huge, and very intimidating. I didn't think I would ever be able to find my way around. I wondered if I would have to ask for directions all the time and become the butt of some upperclassmen's joke. They like to send freshmen the wrong way, and have a laugh at their expense. Now since I was trying so hard to be "Cool" and "Cool" guys don't get lost.

Once I entered the building I was relieved. The layout was pretty simple; Lincoln used to be a hospital during the war times so main access to the upper level was five ramps that were in the center of the building. In between each ramp were hallways lined with lockers and classrooms. At the end of the hallways opposite the ramps was the fire escape. These stairs were available to use if the ramps were too crowded, which was frequently the case since the ramps were a popular hangout spot .The auditorium was in the front of the building, and that was my destination for freshmen orientation.

Once we were all seated, a goofy looking guy with a bird like face introduced himself as the principal. He addressed the class over the shittiest PA system I have ever heard! There were about 900 freshmen, and I don't think he ever had our attention. Everyone was talking, and laughing at Principle big-bird, with his long neck and high water suit pants. I was the only person listening I wanted to hear what he had to say because if there was something that needed to be known I wanted to know, and not have to ask. Remember I wanted to be "Cool".

After principle Big-bird finished addressing the class, we started to break off into homeroom groups. This was done by someone calling out a letter, and if your last name started with that letter then follow that person to your new homeroom.

I finally heard "D" over the loud ruckus. I lined up with about 25 other people and was on my way to my first advisory.

I was excited about advisory I heard stories around the way about how fun it was. The older kids always told us that crazy things happened in advisory. After all these feelings of nervousness, I wanted to have some fun.

We all followed our advisor Dr. Gaines, down the hall. I took this time to survey the rest of the group. It didn't look like a fun bunch, in fact all the good looking girls were back in the auditorium. It seems like only skanks had a last name that began with "D". As we entered the classroom and took a seat, a late comer arrived...a girl. She was FINE!

I lusted after this beauty for **4 long HARD** years. she had the perfect ass, tits, and a face that wasn't beautiful but good-looking.

Unfortunately it didn't seem like I was her type. This girl was fly! She looked like the type that was into guys with money, and plenty of it. But at-least I could fantasize about her.

The guys weren't too impressive either. I was looking around to see whom I could hang with, but it seemed like a class full of dickheads. I wonder if they were thinking the same thing about me?

Advisory was tucked away in a far off corner of the building. It turns out Dr. Gaines was a special ED teacher, which explains why the room was in the back away from everything else. During advisory we received our rosters, and student handbooks, then we got a few words of encouragement a good luck and with that we were dismissed. I managed to talk to a few people; I even chatted briefly with that good-looking beauty, but nothing major. I hadn't developed the finesse that I have now to score points with her.

After dismissal I got my first taste of total bedlam…. The bus ride home.

I was used to a rowdy bus from junior high, and back then I was right in the middle of it. This bus was unlike anything I had ever experienced. The 88 bus would pick us up at the front gate, and it would be packed wall to wall with people. Everyone was cursing, fighting, laughing, pushing and shoving all in the name of fun. There was also the popular entertainment of laughing at the white people.

They would jam the front of the bus, because they were too scared to come to the back. See the back of the bus is where all the cool people, and the rowdiest of the rowdy would sit. If you were cool, you were in the back, and that's where I was. If something was going to go down, I wanted to be right there to see it. In addition I wanted my presence known so that my face was recognizable to the in crowd. I managed to meet a few more people on the bus. No girls unfortunately, but atleast there were a few guys I could talk with.

When I got home all the new high school students got together to discuss their first day. Most of the stories were the same we were all amazed at the women, each of us couldn't wait to get our hands on one of these well-developed beauties. We all looked forward to day 2 which was a full day oh by the way nobody got their ass kicked.

The next day was more exciting than the first; I had the usual roster of freshman classes. 9th grade teachers were nothing memorable. The only one who sticks out in my head was Mr. Curry

Mr. Curry was my algebra teacher. He taught class in the funniest manner, I thought he was very entertaining. He had a big moustache, big black curly hair, and he was always cracking jokes. Even more memorable than him was the vision of loveliness I sat next to in class.

She was a 10th grader, about 5 foot 5 inches, light brown skin, and clearly the most beautiful girl I have ever seen! There was not one imperfection in her face she had a nice slim body and she was FLY! She had the gold jewelry, the newest lee jeans, and the freshest shoes this girl had it going on and I wanted her...BAD

I had a huge crush on this algebra girl. I never revealed my feelings because I didn't think I would even stand a chance. Throughout class we talked, and eventually became good friends.

through talking I found out that she lived kind of close to me. Each morning we would meet up on the bus, and ride to School together I would be fronting hard on the bus acting as if she was my girl. All the guys would look at her because she is so fine and I felt like the man because she was with me or atleast I tried to make it look as if she was with me. I think she knew what I was doing but she never said anything about it.

Anyway Algebra beauty sat in the back of the class with me, and this other girl Gina. I felt good hanging with them in class because I had finally met some women to talk to, but that ended when the bell would ring and we said our good-byes. After Algebra I was headed to lunch.

As I headed for the lunchroom I realized that I didn't know anyone who was going to be in there! I would have to sit alone and look like a jackass. Everyone would look at me, and think what a loser that guy is sitting by himself. At-least that's what I thought they would be thinking. I entered the lunchroom searched for a table that had some guys there, and sat down. Before I knew it they were making conversation with me, before long I had made some buddies.

John and Jared were my first two friends at Lincoln. we would hang together everyday at lunchtime. Through these two I finally figured out how everybody knew each other…they all went to the same junior high school!

There is a junior high right behind Lincoln, and all the kids that went there were sent to Lincoln. That's why I was odd man out! I was one of the only few people who didn't attend JR high with them.

John and Jared knew a lot of people and they introduced me to all the other guys in the lunchroom. After a couple of weeks of hanging out with them I had established my own clique of friends and no longer needed John and Jared.

I was rolling pretty good now, and I had a couple of different groups I would hang out with depending on the day or how I felt. I was full into the high school swing of things; Jason and Jared had now just become faces in the crowd. We barely saw each other anymore or even spoke. I was becoming popular, but not with the ladies. now that I had some boys I was on the look-out to score with the ladies. In addition I wanted to try all the things you do in high school like cut, smoke and drink not necessarily in that order.

I was well into my freshman year when my mother landed a job helping to take care of this old lady. She was making good money now and since it was under the table, she could still collect a welfare check. We were making out like bandits! With the money now rolling in she dropped a bombshell...we were moving!

Not only were we moving but we were moving to the northeast...a white neighborhood? It was like a sentence to **HELL!**

The northeast is full of nothing but whites. I'm not prejudiced, but white people aren't **"DOWN WITH IT"**, and nobody can be **"DOWN"** living in the northeast. Back in those days where you were from was half your rep, now with my year off to a pretty good start I didn't want my rep being tarnished by people thinking I was soft because I lived in this punk ass neighborhood.

I didn't like this one bit! All my friends would be gone! No more football, manhunt or anything. I was losing a big part of my life.

The next month we moved into a nice big two-bedroom apartment in the heart of the northeast. The bathroom was nice and big, with a good tub! I've always had a thing about tubs. In order for me to get in them they must be absolutely clean. This tub was very clean. It was pink, that tub was a dream. Not like the one back in Germantown. That one was all green on the bottom with stains everywhere. No matter how long or hard you scrubbed the stains never came out. I hated that tub. Sometimes I would wear shoes into it when I would shower. These things don't' sound like much, but when you grow up without them when you finally do get them it seems like the greatest thing in the world.

To compound the tragedy I thought living in the northeast was I was the only young person in this new apartment building. We lived in an all-Jewish community, and every person in the complex was atleast 60 years old! We were the only black, under 60 people in the whole place! I missed the old neighborhood already.

Once Monday rolled around I realized one fringe benefit of the move…it only took me 20 minutes to get to school, as opposed to the two hour bus ride it took to get there from Germantown. When I got to algebra class that morning, algebra girl asked me, *"What happened to you this morning?"* she had been looking for me on the bus.

I made up a story, because I didn't want her to know where I was living now. After a couple of days I finally told her that I did-n't' live in the hood anymore, but that I now lived in the northeast. I asked her not to tell anyone. It seems pretty silly now, but back then it was pretty important.

Algebra girl was the only person who knew my secret. After two months of living in this old folks building a young guy and his mother moved into the building. The guy's name was Bob.

Bob had a piece of ass sister named Lynne. Lynne was 18 years old, and fine as shit for a white girl! I would have loved to fuck the shit out of her! I began to hang out with Bob, and this is when the trouble began.

Bob introduced me to the art of graffiti. We used to go out at night, and write graffiti all over the walls around the neighborhood. We met some other guys who were into writing and pretty soon we had our own little posse of wallwriters.

I became obsessed with graffiti! I had it all over my bookbag, television, books, **EVERYTHING!** If there was a space to write on it I did! Bob was our spray paint connection. He had a hookup in his family that would score the paint for us; we got all the free cans we wanted. We possessed everything imaginable that could deface a building, or wall. If I was on a bus or subway I never missed the chance to "tag up". Our hits were everywhere, the bus routes, subway stations, and the El stop. I had even started hitting up in school. We started our own club called F.C.W. (first class writers). Back in the day it was the thing to be in a graffiti club, and I was down with my first one. I was getting a pretty good name in the graffiti world and my tags were starting to get known.

My new found graffiti fame was beginning to cause a problem, and I was beginning to get in trouble over it. We were so into our habit that we started to get sloppy. We started doing stupid things like bombing our own building.

It only took a minute for people to figure out who the culprits were. We were the only kids who lived in the building. Of course we all denied when they accused us. They never had any real proof until one day…

We were all chilling on one of the fire escape balconies in the building. We called this balcony the F.C.W. balcony, because all the members had hit up their name on the door that leads to the balcony. Bob and one of the other guys were sniffing glue. The group except for me had developed a bad habit of huffing this crap! I tried it, but it just wasn't for me. I didn't see what they got out of it. It didn't do anything but make me nauseous. They were up to a four bottle a week habit. So we out there discussing who's wall we were going to kill next, and the maintenance man busts through the door. One of the old bags that lives in the building must have heard us out there, and called him. The old bitches were notorious for causing trouble for us!

Bob smoothly slid the bottle of tywol behind his leg. The only other thing that was going was cigarette smoking, and that's lucky for us. I'm sure that if we'd been smoking anything else he would have called the cops. This guy was poking his nose all around looking for anything he could use to bust our ass! He didn't find anything, he just said angrily that we had to go!

I put up a fight, I screamed at him, **"*WE LIVE HERE! WHY THE FUCK DO WE HAVE TO LEAVE?*"** I didn't really mind leaving; I was just being a wise ass. As we were leaving we all gave him a nice **"Fuck you!"**

As we made our way down the hallway, we were screaming for the old lady who ratted us out to come outside so we could sodomize her! It sounded like a good idea at the time. I led the barrage of cursing; I felt I had the balls to back up anything I said.

We exited the building, and walked along some old train tracks, drank some beer; they sniffed more glue then called it a night. I was glad we didn't hang out late that night I was tired. I had been cutting school and hanging out all day long. I needed to rest up, so I could decide if I was going to school tomorrow.

I had grown quite fond of cutting school. On my report card there were plenty of absences, and I used the same excuse that everyone else does...I just said, *"they messed up!"*

That excuse always works, no matter what! I think it gets handed down from generation, to generation. The funny part is it is true! The school system can never get your attendance right. In high school even before I started cutting there were absences on my report card!

The crew I was hanging with was about to be dismantled; we had a major falling out about three days before Christmas. It was about 2 am and 8 members of F.C.W. including myself were in the lobby of my building. We had just gotten back from a long night of wall writing. We went on an extended 'run' that night.

A 'run' is when you walk an entire bus route, hitting up your name all over. That way every writer that rides the bus will see your tags. That's how you get a rep! Earlier that evening we covered about three bus routes, and we were all beat. So we fall into the lobby, and relax on the sofas.

We were chilling, but being very loud in this conservative building at an ungodly hour. They started huffing glue, and talking about the props we were going to get once daylight hit and our work was seen! I got the bright idea to start break dancing on top of one of the coffee tables. I did a swipe, and hit my leg on the chandelier that hung above the table.

This must have alarmed one of the old hags, because not more than ten minutes later the police came to the door. The front door was made of glass, but locked. The cops could see us, but they couldn't get in. while they were staring at us, Bob stuffs his huff rag in the seat cushion and his bottle under the couch. the cops aren't blind! One of the other dickheads goes over and opens the door to let the police in. what a jackass!

They come right over pull the couch back, find the glue, and threaten to take us downtown. At the thought of that I start bitching. I told them that I live there in the building, where my apartment was, my g.p.a, shoe size any information they wanted to know! This was the first time I had ever been confronted by the police.

Bob, told that he lived in the building too, they hauled us all down to his house, and went to my apartment and got my mother. My mom was cursing up a blue streak! After a lengthy session of lectures, I went upstairs. My mom was livid! I was on punishment for about a week. Needless to say I didn't get anything for Christmas.

After that incident, the guys and me kind of drifted apart. I don't even know why we just did. We didn't go out bombing anymore, or knock on the door for each other. Eventhough my graffiti in the neighborhood had stopped, in school I was going crazy.

Now I was getting a rep in school for writing, and I started hanging with a crew of artists who went to Lincoln. Some of these guys were really good, and I had to practice to perfect my hand. We used to spend all our time comparing each other's styles, and critiquing different pieces. I was now spending my cut time in the lunchroom as opposed to with F.C.W.

I was becoming more belligerent, more flip at the mouth with teachers, and getting to school early to write on the walls. I was out of control wall writing had consumed me.

One day I slipped up, and got caught. I was in environmental science class, and the teacher passed out new textbooks. These books had to be handed in at the end of class. I hated the teacher, and got the bright idea to write her a note on one of the text book pages.

Dear Mrs. Clark,

Fuck you, you fat overweight bitch I can't stand you or your class. when you die I am personally sending a letter to who ever is responsible thanking them for riding the world of you stink ass.

Yours truly,

KASAN

(kasan was my graffiti name)

Not thinking, I had hit up all over the desk I sat at. This was my own personal desk it was all the way at the far end of the classroom alone (I misbehaved sometimes). When the books were passed out the next day some dumbass reported that there was writing in the book.

All the teacher had to do was look at the desktops. I sat alone at my desk, nobody else sat there and it was riddled with **"KASAN"**. I guess she put two and two together and came up with me. I was pulled out of 6 period English class, and taken to the dean's office.

This was my first time in trouble in school. Mr. Pushner was the dean of men. He was a fat bastard who I visited many times in my years at Lincoln. He suspended me right on the spot! Then, he asked to see the rest of my textbooks, which just so happened to be riddled with graffiti. He held them all pending my mother's arrival to reinstate me into school.

I was scared going home. I had to tell my mother I got suspended, and didn't know how to do it. She got home from work at 9:00, and I said she needed to come to school with me the next morning she asked, *"why?"* I said, *"I go suspended for writing a note about my feelings to the teacher"*. I also mentioned that I had to pay for all the textbooks I had written in. She went through the normal routine of yelling, and screaming, and I went through my normal routine of pretending to pay attention. After what seemed like forever, she finally finished. I was sent to my room, and waited for tomorrow.

The next day we got up and went to school. My mother had regained her composure. I guess she did not want to go into the school yelling, and screaming like some mothers (lucky for me). When we got to fat ass Mr. Pusher's office she was calm, and collective. I don't' think that son of a bitch dean liked that, he wanted to see her angry at me. He wanted to see my ass fry! I could see it in his beady little eyes. He told her what happened, and she didn't flip out. I saw him run his fat sausage fingered hands over his butter covered skin, while he waited for her to respond. My mother just wrote a check for the books, and asked him very calmly, *"is there anything else?"* that's when he played his trump card.

I thought I was home free. We were just about to leave his office when that walking cesspool says, *"so how are you doing in your classes?"*

I almost died! Here I was almost out of trouble, and this asshole was opening up a new can of worms. When he saw the look of despair in my eyes a smirk came over his face. He knew he had me, fat ass proceeded to call each, and everyone of my teachers.

When my teachers heard **"MY"** mother was at school, they were more than happy to come down to the dean's office to see her. This way they could tell her in person I was flunking, and hardly attended any classes. They also mentioned that I was the jokester of the classroom, and I would often give a smart remark instead of the answer when I was called on. They told her if I had any chance of passing the 9th grade I would need to ace all of my finals.

This new information got him the response he was looking for. after the parade of teachers left the office and we were dismissed she yanked me out of the dean's office. I was only hoping that she didn't do anything to me that would cause embarrassment infront of my friends…no such luck.

As we were walking to the bus stop, she attempted to slap me in the head. I ducked but unfortunately there was a group of people coming up the pathway. In the group were a few people that knew me, so needless to say I was the subject of smack jokes for the next few weeks. My mother got on the bus, and left. When I got home that day she yelled a whole lot more, and told me if I wanted to continue living…**"I 'D BETTER PASS MY FINALS!"**

After all this trouble I had over the past few weeks I was glad to finally hear some good news…we were moving…again. I was ecstatic, because not only were we moving from whiteytown we were moving back to my old stomping ground…GERMAN-TOWN! We weren't going back to the same block I grew up on, we were going to a more affluent part of G-town into an expensive high rise apartment building. I couldn't wait I was so happy to be leaving the northeast and get back to civilization.

Moving day arrived quickly and the new apartment was even nicer than the old one. It was a really fancy building with a doorman and everything it also had a fully furnished lobby that looked more like a living room of a fancy home than the front of an apartment building. Our place was nice. It was a huge 3 bedroom with 2 bathrooms now I could finally walk through the living room without seeing my sister's face. I had my own large room as well with a phone! A phone in my room this was a major score now I could get my social life started.

Now that I was back around the way I started hanging out with one of my old buddies from junior high…Derek.

Derek and I became really close. We would talk on the phone for hours, he was always at my house or I was at his we were true buddies.

I can remember one day we both cut school over his house, and tried weed for the first time. I supplied the pot (which I stole from my mom), but I only had enough paper to roll one joint. We each wanted our own joint, because neither one of us wanted to smoke after the other. After I rolled my joint in strawberry flavored top paper (also stolen from my mother) Derek took the excess weed, and rolled it up in loose-leaf paper bound together with scotch tape.

When I saw this giant joint that looked like something from a Cheech and Chong movie I couldn't stop laughing. I wasn't even high, but you would have thought I was. I doubled over on the ground cracking up! Derek kept standing there with this giant joint made of loose-leaf paper puffing away! He looked like such an idiot, but the laughter stopped when we heard the front door opening!

Both of our hearts stopped dead!

Not only were we smoking weed, but it was 10 o'clock in the morning. We both should have been in school. When we heard that door turn we tossed the pitifully rolled joints over the balcony down into the bushes. Derek grabbed a can of air-freshener, and began to spray frantically!

We stood there as nonchalantly as possible waiting to see who it was coming in the door. We figured we could make up a lie about being home from school, but there was no excuse for the weed smell that was still all over us!

We both stood motionless, and ready to shit our pants, because we both think it's going to be his mother coming through the door. When the door finally opened up it revealed the face of Derek's dumb ass older brother Myron.

Myron was about 5 years older than Derek, and was the biggest fucking nerd I had ever met. He was a wannabe rapper/homeboy who was about as down as peewee Herman. This guy was a real cornball he was a brainiak who attended one of those specially gifted high schools. all I know is I was glad it wasn't his mother.

Myron immediately smelled the pot smoke and says, *"I know yall were in here smoking!"* we denied it and said, *"we don't know what you are talking about!"*. He told us, *"Man, I get high ALL the time! "I just don't do it inside the house, That way nobody will be able to catch me!"*

There's no way I believed that story from this nerd! I just wanted him to hurry up and finish talking so he could get the fuck out of our business. After his attempt to convince us he was cool he went upstairs. Strange thing is he never asked us what we were doing there, and I was glad of that. I guess he figured we were there, and we shouldn't have been, and he was there and shouldn't have been so why make waves.

After Myron was upstairs for 20 minutes he came back down, and left without a word. I guess he forgot his science experiment, and came home to get it. Nevertheless I was glad he was gone, I didn't really like him. After we regained our composure I was upset that we had wasted our perfectly good joints, because of this asshole.

Derek and me had tons of adventures like the time we got locked up!

It was a Friday night Derek and I were in his room totally bored. So we decided to goto the mall and catch a movie. When we got to the theater there wasn't' anything good playing so, we cruised the mall for girls. Both of us struck out so now we were going to shop. We went into one of the large department stores, and got the bright idea to steal some cologne.

We walked around this large store, and we didn't see any security guards. So we went to the fragrance aisle, and loaded up! I had like 4 bottles in my coat pocket, and he took 2.

We started to head to the exit. As we were about to step through the exit we started high fiving each other because it looked like we were going to get away with it. We got out of the store and walked up the ramp when two plain clothed security guards came up behind us and grabbed our arms flashed a badge and told us we were caught!

We were so close to getting away, Before these guys came up. I was thinking about going back in to get more stuff. They took us to the back of the store, and pulled the goods out of our pockets. Derek was being a smart-ass, telling jokes, and giving the rental cops a hard time. I on the other hand turned into a complete bitch!

I was so scared! I couldn't even write my name down on the paper, because my hands were shaking so badly. Because Derek was being a smart-ass they called the real cops, who cuffed us and took us to **JAIL!**

I WAS SHITTING BRICKS! When that squad car pulled up in the station house. Once inside the station house we were stripped of our personal possessions, and led to a tiny cell. All our info on how to contact our parents was written down by a smart-ass cop who sat behind a giant desk.

Derek gave his real information, and I gave fake information. I was hoping I could convince Derek's mom to take me home, If she did my mother would never know what happened. While waiting for his Mom to show we were put in separate cells. It was a small cage with a slab of wood hanging off the wall for use as a bed. the toilet was in the middle of the floor without any partitions around it for privacy. I definitely did not want to be here.

After about an hour Derek's mom showed up. I could hear her chewing out Derek in the other room. I was standing at my bars like a puppy in a kennel looking to see if she was going to take me. After a few minutes the yelling stopped, and I heard doors closing.

"I CAN'T BELIEVE IT THAT BITCH LEFT ME HERE!"

His mother told them to call my mother, because she wasn't taking me anywhere! I was screaming for the cops to let me talk to her, but they wouldn't. I had no choice; I broke down and gave them my real information.

We didn't have a car, so they sent a squad car to pick up my mother. When she arrived at the station house, the faggot cop on duty finally let me out of that tiny cell. I was led down a long hallway that emptied into the booking room. I stood face to face with my mother, and I could tell by the look in her eyes that she was beyond angry. If I was going to get out of this one, I was going to have to come up with something good.

The wheels of thought began to turn violently in my head, and I came up with a long shot. This was not a time to rely on a far-fetched idea, but my time was short, so I decided to try it. I told her that *"I needed to talk because I felt that nobody listened to me, and I didn't feel important"*. I was laying it on thick, and under the circumstances I had no choice. I followed up with a nice line that *"I was hurting inside!"*

This was probably one of the biggest lines of bullshit that I ever laid out in my life. I must have been pretty convincing because it worked. I had my mom totally fooled! She started to break down and became teary eyed. She started hugging me, now when this happened I knew I had escaped.

Not only did I not get yelled at, but I didn't get any type of punishment either. This was a narrow escape! Derek wasn't so lucky, he was on punishment, and his mother forbid him to see me. He told her it was all my idea to steal the cologne, and that I pushed him to do it!

Derek would always try to blame someone else to save his own ass. We kept in phone contact, but we didn't hang together for a long while after that incident.

Derek and I didn't hook up again for about a month. I just came over his house one Saturday, and his mom let me in. he was about to go out to the movies with a couple of his friends, and some girl so I told him, *"I would catch up with him later"*. The girl he was meeting at the movies was Shante.

Shante and Derek had been talking on the phone for a few weeks. He met her over the phone while over some guy's house she went to school with. She called and Derek took the phone and just started kicking game to her. We were always doing shit like that. I guess she went for what he was saying because they exchanged numbers and had been talking for a little while, and were finally going to meet face to face.

I met up with Derek after they got back from the flick and I asked him, *"how did it go?"*

He said, *"it was the pits"*. Derek told me that they all went to 69th street to the movies. When he saw Shante she was white as a ghost, skinny, and ugly. When they went in the theater he said he didn't want to sit next to her so she sat next to one of the other guys that went. He claimed it was a total waste of his time. Now Derek was my closest friend, but I knew he was a bullshitter. If this was his story, the truth was still out there somewhere else. I knew if I wanted the real deal I needed to speak to someone else that was on the trip.

On my way home I stopped at Devin's house. Devin just so happened to be someone who went on this trip. I wanted the real scoop. And he gave it to me!

I told Devin the fairytale Derek told me, and he bust out laughing! Turns out Derek wanted Shante, but she was not having it! Derek was my man, but he also was a **BIG UGLY MOTHERFUCKER!** Devin went on to tell me that she did sit next to Derek, but he must have sensed that she didn't like him, so he started a fight with her (typical Derek). That's the reason why she moved.

Needless to say Derek and Shante stopped talking after that day. I told Derek that I had found out the real story, but he still denied it. That was the end of the Derek and Shante romance. But the beginning of ours...

Next week while at Devin's house the phone rang...it was Shante. When Derek found this out he started to yell, and talk shit about her. These two went back and forth insulting each other over the phone.

Finally, I grabbed the phone and was like, *"what's up? Why are you so hostile with my boy?"*

She said, *"I'm not trying to be mean, but he started with me!"* The conversation ended up with me calling her a bitch, and telling her not to call anymore! Then I hung up the phone.

When I got home that evening the phone rang and it was Shante! I was like **"How did you get my number?"** she said, *"I got it from Devin"*. We immediately started to insult each other and eventually stopped the insults and started talking. She called at around 8 p.m. and we didn't hang up until 7 a.m. the next morning!

The only reason we got off the phone is because I had to goto school and take finals. We talked about everything that night. I couldn't believe how interesting she was. Shante was exactly the opposite of everything that Derek said and what I thought. I was seeing a different side of her now she was a sweet girl and I was beginning to like her...a lot!

I wanted to stay on the phone and talk with her forever, but I had finals. I told her I would call her from school after my first test was over.

The dreaded day was finally here, I was so nervous about taking my finals. I kept hearing the voices of all my teachers' words echoing over and over that if I didn't pass all my tests that I was sure to repeat the 9th grade. I could only afford to fail one class and still pass if I failed more than one I was doomed to repeat! I knew that my grades weren't that good since I became fond of cutting. The final counts as one third of your final grade, I just hoped the "B's that I earned from the first report period would carry me through this rough time, on top of all this I remembered my mother's threat. Now I wasn't nervous…I was scared!

The ride to school for me was a pretty somber one I felt like a man on the way to the gas chamber. When I arrived I went to the lunchroom to see who was there. I seemed to be the only guy in the group nervous about finals, I chatted with them for a brief moment the bell rang and we all scattered to get to class. The first final for me was environmental science, I knew that bitch Mrs. Clark was going to make it a tough one. I often wondered if she harbored any resentment towards me for the note I wrote her if she did secretly hate me she never showed it in class, but it turns out she did get revenge in the end.

After an hour and a half of endless question answering I finally finished the test. I felt pretty confident that I had aced it. As I walked out of her classroom I was glad I would never have to deal with that fat bitch again. A smirk came over my face because I figured it would be like a slap in the face to her because I knew she wanted me to fail I thought, 'I'll show her'.

When final test results were posted environmental science final exam grade...**80**.

Each day consisted of 2 final exams one at 8, and the other at 10. There was a half four break in between to relax. I headed for my usual spot the lunchroom. Through all the tension I almost forgot about the call I needed to make to Shante. So I raced to the phone in the lunchroom before anyone else got on it. Before I dialed her number I wondered 'Does she really like me the way I like her?' was last night a fluke? If I call this early will she think I'm sweating her? Would she be angry for me ringing her phone this early? I debated for a few more minutes and came to the conclusion to call. The phone rang twice and a sleepy voiced Shante answered.

When she picked up the phone I was a little apprehensive to speak because she sounded so tired, and I expected to get yelled at but the exact opposite happened once I said hello she immediately recognized my voice and told me she was glad I called. She asked me how I thought I did on my final? Shante made me feel special because she seemed like she really cared about me. We talked for about 10 minutes, then a line started to form at the phone, and my buddies noticed I was talking on the phone so they came over to see if I was speaking to a female. Once they found out it was a girl the teasing began, so I had to hang up. Before we got off the phone we made plans to meet today after school.

After I got off the phone I was on cloud 9. I was about to have a girlfriend! I floated on air to the table where all the guys were seated; I was brought back to reality when they started talking about the next test. My stomach started to do double back flips. In a couple of hours I was going to see Shante, and in a couple of minutes I was going to take my next final. The same thoughts kept going through my head: What if she didn't like me? What if she thought I was ugly?

We clicked so well over the phone I didn't want to lose her like Derek did! I hadn't even told him that I started talking to her. I wonder what he would think if it worked out between me and Shante?

One thing is for certain if she thinks I'm ugly, and doesn't want to be bothered with me...I'll never tell him. The embarrassment of that would be too great, but if she likes me then boy am I going to rub it in his face! My daydream was broken by the shrill sound of the bell for the next class...algebra 1.

Mr. Curry was in a particularly festive mood. He was cracking jokes as soon as the students started to pile through his door. I wasn't extra nervous about this exam, because ever since I got in trouble about the text books my seat had been moved to the front of the class and I had been really paying attention.

The paper and pencils were passed out I opened the book and began. The test was a breeze way easier than I could have ever imagined I was finished in an hour without a hitch...Algebra 1 final exam grade: **86**.

Now with today's set of finals out of the way I was about to tackle the real test my meeting with Shante. As I walked to the bus stop I was in a daze if this girl didn't like me I would be crushed.

We agreed to meet at the bus depot, which was about a 30-minute ride for me on the 88 bus. All my boys were looking at me and wondering what was up? Why was I acting like somebody died? I hadn't' told them about Shante, because if It didn't work out I didn't want to look like a fool. As the bus pulled into the terminal I was woozy! It felt like I could throw up at any minute.

As coolly as I could, I needed to check myself over before I got off that bus. I looked at my reflection in the window to make sure that my hair and clothes were perfect (which they were). Then I needed the breath test. I cupped my hand over my mouth and blew out, then I deeply inhaled. It smelled like roses, everything seemed as good as it was going to get.

I exited the bus when it pulled to a stop, and in my hippest homeboy stroll I ambled over to the agreed meeting spot. As I made my way closer, and closer to the corner we were supposed to meet, I spotted her from behind. I was able to recognize her because she told me what she was going to be wearing.

Ill never forget that day, she had on a blue denim skirt with a tight fitting white shirt, and the current craze in footwear white filas. I looked her up and down and I couldn't believe it.

Shante was FINE, atleast from behind. I hadn't even made my way to see her face yet, and she was already the most beautiful girl in the world to me. When I finally did get closer she turned around and I was not disappointed.

This girl was cute! She had light skin with cute little freckles all over her cheeks, and big brown eyes. **Shante was FINE!** This was good but also bad. A girl this fine might not want me is what I began to think, all I could hope is that I was wrong.

I strolled up to her in my black lee jeans, white polo shirt and my spanking new white filas. I struck a pose and said, *"You are Shante.... Right?"*. I paid close attention to her facial expression when she looked at me for the first time. No matter what she said this would really tell the story of if she liked me or not. She looked me up, and down and began to smile. I let out a huge sigh of relief.

We stood on that corner and talked for about 20 minutes. I was so happy; I passed my most important test today. **she liked me she really liked me!** I wanted to jump for joy but I managed to keep my composure.

Shante had to get back home because she had to baby-sit her little sister who would be home from school soon. She asked me if I would see her home and of course I said an emphatic *"YES!"*

We boarded the "EL" train, and sat in the last car. I chose this car so we would be away from all my friends that took the train home too. I knew they wouldn't be in the last car because all the cool people sit in the first car. Don't ask me why, but on the train it's cool to sit in the front, on the bus it's the back.... Go figure!

Shante was too new of an acquaintance to be around my friends yet. I wanted to make sure she was going to be around before I was seen here and there with her.

We sat down, and cozied up to each other. The conversation flowed as well in person as it did on the phone. When we talked she would always look me right in the eyes. I hated that; back then I had a huge problem making eye contact during a conversation. She kept staring right into my eyes and it was really making me uncomfortable, but she kept doing it...Hey, maybe she REALLY liked me.

As we were riding along she said something that was way out of left field...she asked me, *"are you going to kiss me?"*. I was shocked! I hadn't' kissed a girl in over a year! The graduation trip was the last time my lips had met a female non-relative. That kiss on the bus from Annapolis was nothing; this was going to be a real kiss with a potential love interest. I responded with a sheepish *"yes"* and she said, *"Well, do it then!"*

Now as I prepared to kiss this beauty I only hoped that I had some skills. I had practiced on pillows, and stuffed animals but this was the real deal! As I tilted my head to the right ever so slightly, and began to move my freshly moistened lips closer to hers the most perfect thing in the world happened...Just as our lips touched, the lights went out on the train.

I couldn't' believe it this must have been a message from up above that this was the girl for me. I was in heaven as our tongues wrestled with each other, and her strawberry scented breath filled my mouth and nostrils. I could've stayed frozen in time like that for all eternity.

As we broke our kiss the lights came back on (this is true believe it or not). We spent the rest of the train ride talking about the kiss; she was very pleased with it (needless to say).

When the train arrived at the end of the line it was time to get off. Shante lived on the other side of town in a section called Wynnefield.

Wynnefield is on the edge of the city limits. It's a long bus ride from where I lived. It was worth it to me, because I got to spend so much time with her. Once we exited the train we had to catch another bus that would take us the final distance home.

When we finally reached her house, and I didn't want to leave her. I wanted to come in, and stay for a while but that was a no-no. Shante's parents didn't play that. We kissed goodbye, and I went home. As soon as I got in the house I rushed to the phone and called Derek.

I gloated to him how Shante and me met over the phone, and in person. He said he didn't care, but their seemed to be a little bit of hurt in his voice. Derek stood by his alleged feelings of hate for her, and that he thought she was ugly. No matter what he said I know he wished that it was him that hit it off with her.

The two of them continued their hatefest throughout the entire relationship. Neither ever had a kind word to say to the other. I was both of their friends, so I was always stuck trying to be the peacemaker. After talking with Derek, I called Shante.

I really shouldn't have been on the phone, because I had finals the next morning and I needed to pass. We still put in and all night session of talking only this time we ended at 5 am.

The next couple of days blew by. I kicked ass on every final except world history. I barely showed up for that class, and when I did all I did was look at the clock waiting for the bell to ring. I don't think I ever passed a test in that class. World history was the only class I knew I failed. So by the fail one-class definition, I should be a 10th grader next year. Hopefully that would be the case, but I would have to wait for my report card to be mailed out over the summer before I was certain.

With school done now comes another summer. only this time I have something I never had in the summer…a girlfriend.

I spent the entire vacation hanging out with Derek, or on the phone with Shante sometimes I did both. Shante's parents wouldn't let her out of the house much, which is why we spent so much time on the phone. If she went to the bathroom, I went with her. If I was taking a shower, she went with me, we were inseparable.

We worked out a plan for secret phone calls since our parents often tried to keep us off it. If one of these instances would occur, we synchronized our watches, and agreed upon a time that one of us would call the other. About one minute before that time one of us would call time, and wait for the other line to click. When it did you could just click over and begin talking. That way the phone wouldn't ring, and nobody would know we were on it.

The first time Shante, and I went out on a date we had to take her little sister. We all went to the mall, and a movie. Since her parents didn't know that I was going I had to meet them at the bus stop. Her little sister was cute, but young. We talked on the phone sometimes and she liked me, which is why I knew she wouldn't tell I was going on this outing. We met at the "EL" stop I was glad to see my baby again even if she had her tag along sister in tow.

Shante and I managed to get a little bit of private conversation in before her little sister started to try to monopolize the conversation. She was a little obnoxious, but we had to put up with it because if we didn't she would surely tell her parents that I had came on this trip.

I had begun to notice something strange through phone conversations with her sister, and now I was actually seeing that she had a crush on me! She kept looking at me, and I could swear she had lust in her eyes!

Her sister was 10 years old, and she was looking at me like a horny old lady! It made me a little uncomfortable but we had arrived at the movie house so I figured the picture would distract her from thoughts of me.

I paid for the tickets, and we got seated. Now I thought little sis would watch the movie while I sneak feels of Shante's tits…**NOT**.

Her sister sat next to me instead of next to Shante. Once the movie started I figured I would give it about 10 minutes before I started getting my feel on. As I sat in the chair, and was just about to start doing my thing I felt a little hand caressing my ass! This was nice only one problem…It wasn't Shante's hand it was her **SISTER'S!**

This little girl was feeling me up in the goddamn Movie Theater! I was shocked and didn't know how to react. First, I tried to ignore it hoping that she would stop on her own…no such luck. I leaned over and whispered in Shante's ear that her sister was grabbing my ass. Shante leaned over and asked her, *"where are* *your hands?"*. This little girl ignored her, and kept fondling me! She wouldn't stop! **This horny kid was hell-bent on making love to my ass with her hand!**

Finally, Shante moved her sister on the other side of her, and spent the rest of the movie tending to her sister. **What a fucking waste!**

I was expecting to get some feels, and instead I got an ass massage from a 10-year-old! What a fucked up day!

The next time we got to go out was a few weeks later. Shante's cousin Sandra was visiting for a couple of weeks and she managed to convince her parents to let them out of the house. We planned to make a double date out of it I got Derek to come along as a date for her cousin. I had never seen Sandra but I told Derek she was fine. He told me, *"if she looks anything like Shante I'm going to slap the shit out of her and leave!"*. I reassured him that she was fine, and hoped that she was so there wouldn't be any drama. I finally got him to agree to go I'm surprised he did since he seemed to hate Shante.

Once all the particulars were set we met up on a Saturday at the train station I had to beg Shante not to tell her what Derek looked like so she wouldn't scare her away. If Derek and Sandra hit it off I would be able to get in some scoring with Shante. On the way to meet the girls, I was hyping up the situation by filling Derek's head with the idea of how fine Sandra is going to be! I could tell by the way he was acting that he was starting to believe me when I said she was fine. Derek was anxious and couldn't wait to see her.

As the train pulled into the station I saw Shante on the platform she looked as beautiful as ever I swear that everytime I saw that girl she was even prettier than the last time. We made eye contact and I motioned to her before the doors closed to get back on the train so we didn't have to wait for the next one.

The train was crowded so Eventhough I saw Shante I didn't have a chance to get a first look at Sandra. The train began to move and we had to walk through 3 cars to get to our women so I looked at Derek and said, *"lets' go get them!"* Derek couldn't hide the big Kool-Aid grin that broke out on his face in his mind he knew he was on his way to meet the finest girl on the planet. As we made our way through the cars I was catching glimpses of Derek checking himself out in the reflection from the windows to make sure he was playa perfect.

We finally made it to the front door of the car the girls were in and before I opened the door I paused for a minute took a deep breath and stepped in. Shante and Sandra were standing right by the door. Shante was decked out in some tight fitting stretch jeans and a nice white form-fitting shirt that showcased her lovely breasts. Sandra was standing to her right she wasn't bad a nice light chocolate sister in tight blue jeans that showed off a juicy ass she was cute too she was no Shante but if I didn't have a girl already I would have talked to her. I was hoping that these two would like each other I greeted Shante with a toothy smile and introduced my boy Derek to Sandra.

I could see disappointment on the faces of both girls, and once Sandra looked directly at Derek her face frowned up even more like she just drank a glass of sour milk I looked at Derek and this guy had the same look as they did. This was not turning out the way I planned.

We all took a seat. I sat next to Shante, Derek and Sandra sat down reluctantly next to each other. The tension in the air was thick! I tried to lighten things up with a little casual conversation, but somehow the talking turned to insults.

I heard Sandra whisper to Shante, *'Why did RJ, bring this ugly motherfucker?'.* I wasn't the only one who heard this poor attempt at a whisper; Derek heard it as well. This guy now raised his voice as loud as he could and said, ***"Bitch you ain't cute!"***

That was it! Sandra and Shante began a nonstop verbal assault on Derek. They talked about everything, from his corny aviator sunglasses, to his hat, down to his shoes. Derek tried to attack back, but they were relentless. I didn't know what to do! I tried to get them to all shut up, but it was way out of control. The **'fuck-yous, and suck-my-dicks'** were flying back and forth a mile a minute! I was glad our stop was next, because this was beginning to get embarrassing!

As we stepped off the train Derek screamed at the top of his lungs **"FUCK YOU BITCH"** and stormed off! All the people on the platform were staring at us. We were all stunned and stood there with our mouths open. I couldn't believe this guy left! Sandra and Shante were glad he was gone, but all I could think was *"**DAMN**, I'm never going to get my hands on this girl!".*

After Derek split we decided not to goto the movies; we went downtown instead to walk around the mall. I think Sandra was attracted to me because she kept looking at me and walking really close to me. I remember thinking to myself that if she starts to feel my ass my lips are sealed. I guess Shante picked up on this because she asked me to put Sandra to the test.

Shante and I were standing in the doorway of some clothing store while Sandra looked around inside Shante looked at me and said, *"I think she likes you"*. I knew this was true but I played the dumb role and gave her a don't be ridiculous look.

Shante wanted me to go into the store and feel Sandra's butt to see what she would do. I wanted to do this more than anything in the world what an opportunity this would be to touch that glorious ass I declined though because Eventhough my mind said, **"HELL YES!"**. I knew it would cause trouble in my new-found relationship.

We continued with our day of window shopping, and talking the conversation often came back to the situation with Derek even if he was my man it was still funny I tried to stick up for him in-between all the jokes at his expense

Now it was getting late, so I had to take them back home I gave Shante a kiss goodbye as I left them at the 52nd street "EL" stop. As I rode the train home I was disappointed another date and I still didn't get the chance to score with Shante I was getting more than a little frustrated. When I got home before I called Shante I phoned Derek.

Derek was like "***WHY DID YOU SET ME UP WITH THAT UGLY BITCH?***" I was like, *"**she is not ugly you two just got stupid on each other!**"* I told him about how I had the chance to feel her butt. He laughed and said, *"if my girl would have told me to grip her butt, my hands would have been all over it!"* I guess that's why he 's single. I got Derek to admit that Sandra was good looking, and had a fat ass. I knew he wanted her, he only started talking shit because they didn't like him. I ended our conversation so I could call my baby.

Throughout the remainder of the summer Shante and I got more and more hot with each other over the telephone. Our conversations continued to get dirtier and dirtier by the day. We were both extremely anxious to experiment sexually with each other. Shante was a virgin, and so was I and we both wanted to see what it felt like to do it. Not only did we want to do it we wanted to do it all she talked about how her girlfriends told her that it felt good to be eaten. I never ate a girl or even thought about it, but for Shante I would have tried anything.

Since she brought up the topic of eating I came back with how good it would feel to get a blowjob! We both agreed to do each other. Now it was set, we knew what we were going to do we just needed an opportunity to do it.

Shortly after our talk we got our chance Shante pulled off a miracle and got to go out on a date without her sister and on top of that her parents knew she was going out with me!

Labor Day weekend we were on to goto the movies by ourselves and my plan was to do all the things we had talked about.

I arrived at her house in the early afternoon walked slowly up the stairs and rang the bell I had never met her parents before they knew of me from our constant phone activity but this was the first face to face meeting!

Shante greeted me at the door, and she looked a little nervous. I stepped inside, and surveyed the house. It was nice, her family lived in an upper middle class neighborhood, so I didn't expect it to be a shit hole inside but it was better than I had anticipated. I took two steps down, and I was in a sunken living room with a huge couch at the far end of the wall. Seated on the couch was her father, he immediately got up and started to walk towards me.

He was a short man with thinning curly black hair, not an intimidating looking man but I was intimidated. I could see on his face that he wasn't too crazy about me taking his daughter out. I was kind of glad her mother wasn't home I felt very uncomfortable and wanted to get out of there as soon as possible. After a little small talk and a private watch this guy talk with his daughter Shante and I were off we could hardly keep our hands off each other while we waited for the bus were kissing and fondling all over the place. When we got to the movies it couldn't have been more perfect there were only about five people in the theater with nobody in the back row, which is right where we took a seat and got ready for the festivities to begin.

As we settled in our seats the reality of what was about to happen started to hit us and we got a case of the nerves. I was beginning to think that I was going to chicken out Shante looked at me and asked me, *"Do you have a condom?"*. Of course I had a condom! I had been waiting for this moment the whole summer she looked me right in the eye and asked me, *"Do you remember what you said you were going to do?"* I remembered and proceeded.

I bent down on one knee in front of her put her legs up on either side of the armrests lifted her dress and plunged my tongue deep inside her womanhood. I had prepared myself for this to be one of the nastiest tastes in the world, but instead it tasted sweet. Not just sweet, but down right good! I licked, sucked, and slurped for what seemed like hours. I couldn't believe how good it was, and it was fun too I looked up at Shante and saw her head rolling around. I also liked to hear the gasps of pleasure that escaped from her partially parted lips. The look of pleasure on her face set me off even more! It made my tongue work faster, and explore every crevice of her sweet teen pussy. I had no experience in cunnilingus, but I think I was performing like a pro that day. It was an extreme turn on to be able to give someone this amount of pleasure! It made me crazy seeing how hot it made her to be eaten. My face was covered in pussy juice, and I lapped up every bit of it! Shante was soaked and I knew I did a good job.

I got up and sat on the chair because it was my turn now I slipped my pants down and my dick was rock hard I didn't have any trouble with limp dick this time. She grabbed my rock hard dick, and was looking at it for a long time. I was holding my breath in anticipation of feeling her lips wrap around my hot rod. She finally opened up, and sank my head into her virgin mouth…for about 10 seconds. Then she stopped, and told me to put the condom on she was going to ride me.

10 seconds of head what a gip! I ripped the condom open and rolled it down my elongated shaft Shante lifted her skirt and got on top of me I plunged deep inside her and the feeling was magnificent! It was so tight and wet then she started to move her ass up and down slowly on my rigid dick. She leaned forward a bit, and started to pick up speed. Shante was moaning, groaning, and she began to call out my name!

This was incredible, at that moment I knew I was hooked on pussy for life! All of a sudden my body got tense my legs got rigid and…the theater door opened! Just as I was about to explode the action had to stop. Two ladies with about three kids came in and sat right the fuck in front of us of all the goddamn empty seats in the place they had to come sit directly in front of me!

Shante got off my dick and we took a break for a moment. Just for a moment because we started up kissing and touching each other again I guess they sensed our horniness because they got up and moved to the other side of the theater. Once they left, she got right back ontop of my dick. While she rode me I kept looking over at the ladies, and they were checking us out fucking. This got me even more hot knowing that they were watching us fuck! I started to pump harder, the ladies provided extra stimulation, and before I knew it I was pumping a hot load of cum into the condom.

She got off and we watched the rest of the movie We were both spent of energy and sat in silence on the way home when we talked on the phone that evening all we could discuss was the fact that we were no longer virgins.

School was now just a couple of days away and I began to worry if I had passed to the tenth grade since I never received my report card in the mail I had no idea what my final grades turned out to be. If I failed it would be the ultimate embarrassment to be a freshman again what would my mother say? Certainly she would be very disappointed failure or not I'll find out in one day because the first day of school is tomorrow. I had a fine girl, and was no longer a virgin what could go wrong?

That evening Shante and me kept the conversation short. She was nervous about starting high school, and I was nervous about returning. I didn't tell her that I might be stuck back in the 9th grade again. In fact I didn't tell anyone not even Derek. I wished her good luck, and went to bed; hopefully I'll be a sophomore.

I had forgotten how long of a bus ride it was from Germantown to Lincoln. As I boarded the 88 bus I started to see all my old school buddies. I looked at all the new freshmen getting on the bus for their first time. It's not hard to tell who they are; they all have the same wide-eyed look like I did my first day. I didn't speak to them at all I was an upperclassman, and couldn't be bothered with freshmen. When we arrived at Lincoln, all the guys and me stood at the front gate rating the new crop of females.

It seemed like a nice crop of fresh meat now that I wasn't a virgin anymore I was anxious to try my newfound sexual prowess with them.

The bell rang that meant it was time to goto my old advisory and find out my new book number, hopefully it would be a 10th grade one. I went to the room, and saw my goofy old advisor. She had that same stupid ass look that she did last year! She instantly remembered me, and greeted me with a friendly *"Hello"* I returned her hello, no other words were necessary because she knew why I was there.

She looked at her records, and found my name. That's when my worst fear came true. I was in book 406 again! **I GOT LEFT DOWN!**

I couldn't believe it! My face was in total shock. I started to rethink every grade I got last year to see where I could have failed.

She showed me my report card, and as I moved down the list of classes I saw everything that I expected. I had all passing grades except for world history. That grade was an "E", as expected. Then the last one floored me environmental science…**"E".**

THAT FAT BITCH FAILED ME!

I marched right up to her room to ask her fat ass about my bull-shit grade.

I stormed up the stairs, and marched right into her room. Jabba was sitting at her desk. I looked her right in the eye and said, *"You, failed me, and I'm interested in knowing why!"* I had a high "C" average going into the last report period Eventhough I didn't do shit the final marking period, but ace the final. the hard work I did in the beginning of the year should have pulled me through. I averaged it out over and over in my mind and there was no fuck-ing way I could have failed. That bitch pulled out her book and smugly told me that in the 1st marking period I worked very hard and when grading time came around I had a high **"C"** average so she gave me two points and I got a **"B"** for the first quarter. She then stated the rest of the year I didn't do anything so she **TOOK BACK THE POINTS!** That fat pumpkin stomach bitch did it to get back at me, I know she did! How the fuck can she take back a grade from the beginning of the year to make me fail at the end of the year? She didn't take it back when I wasn't doing shit in the 2nd or 3rd period, why in the 4th? That plump bitch had figured a way to get the last laugh! I still hate that cow to this day.

I can't believe it 9th grade all over again and there wasn't a thing I could do about. I had to hide this from everyone! Oh god! If anyone found out about this I would be so embarrassed. Most of all I had to keep it from my mother! I didn't know how I was going to do it, but I had to be an angel this year. I couldn't get into a lick of trouble, because if I did she would find out for certain. I needed to buckle down this year and pass all my classes with flying colors, and goto summer school to make up for last years catastrophe. I vowed to myself to do it. It wouldn't be easy but I was going to make it happen.

It started out right away not being easy. As soon as I walked by the dean's office, that fat bastard Mr. Pushner looked up from his desk and called me in. he wanted a copy of my roster so he could know where I was at all times. I saw the smirk on his face when he saw I was in the 9th grade again. He photocopied my roster and told me he would be watching me.

I hadn't even been in the building for 20 minutes and already I was being watched. I was depressed all day I noticed that plenty of my friends had been left down and they didn't seem to care to me this was the most humiliating thing that could have happened I was so ashamed.

I went home that day and Shante told me all about her first day in high school she was very excited and told me every little detail I told her about my day too ofcourse I left out the little detail about me flunking.

Staying out of trouble made the year breeze by quickly I managed to keep my nose clean and keep the secret about me flunking from my friends. In the 9th grade classes I had I told the freshmen I was a sophomore, and failed this class last year and in my 10th grade classes I acted like I was one of them. The only people who knew were the teachers, and they never mentioned it. So my secret was safe.

When report card time came around I just didn't tell my mother she never knew when report cards were issued so she never asked. I did show her one report card so she wouldn't be suspicious and this is when I became creative with bleach and a felt tip pen it's amazing how "D's" can miraculously be transformed into "B's" with those materials all was fine with me except for one thing…Shante.

Shante and I had been together for about 8 months now and at that age that was an eternity. I was totally head over heels in love with her! I would have married her if I could have. We would meet downtown just about every day, just so we could ride the bus home together. While on the bus we would do some heavy kissing, and exploring of each other's bodies. I became more and more experienced with the art of pussy eating and she got more practice at fellatio. We would do everything on the bus except fuck. There were hundreds of times when the bus was packed with people and a bookbag or coat would be covering up me getting jerked off everything seemed to be going great.

One day I got home from school and Shante dropped a bomb on me…she wanted out of the relationship. I was crushed my heart was breaking I did everything imaginable for this girl and now she wanted to dump me why? How could this be happening? It turns out that everyday after she got out of school, some guy would wait for her. She would tell him; *"I'm on my way to meet my boyfriend"* she would ignore whatever he was saying. Eventually he got her to take his number, and she called him. They started talking and now she wanted out with me so she could be in with him. I was devastated I tore my room apart and was depressed for weeks. I was totally in love with her and this is how she treated me. I swore to her that I would hate her forever. She didn't care she had a new man and I was just a memory

I was alone now and it felt like my world was collapsing around me of all things don't you know the guy she left me for was named Derek...

I didn't want to do much of anything after we broke up I just went to school and came home and moped in my room. I didn't tell anyone that we broke up I just stayed to myself after a few weeks of self pity I finally started to come back to reality I began hanging out with Derek and joining the ranks of the living.

We are moving again! Yes again, we moved so much in my childhood that it seemed normal to me to move once a year. This time we were moving to a house, I was excited this would be the first house I ever lived in. there was only one problem it was deep in the heart of North Philly.

North Philly at that time was one of the roughest parts of the city and we were moving to 26th and Allegheny the roughest of the rough ontop of this my brother was moving back in and Merrill was coming too.

Merrill had become a close friend of the family and he was having problems with his mother and when he asked my mom if he could stay with us ofcourse she said yes. We moved into a 3 bedroom house right on Allegheny avenue there was plenty of activity on this block all illegal this was at the height of people getting robbed for gold chains and sneakers and this seemed to happen daily on this block. The neighborhood was as rough as you could imagine! Crack sellers, and smokers lined every corner looking to buy or sell. Fights and gunshots were common place as well as prostitutes. I was a little scared at first, but the fear quickly wore off. I became very comfortable with this hostile environment. There were about 2 weeks of school left and this nightmarish year would finally be over.

Summer school sucked! how could it not suck? Sitting in school when it was ninety degrees outside, and one hundred degrees in the classroom! The school was full of fine looking bitches, but not in any of my classes. I was stuck in summer school taking world history, which I failed my 1st time around 9th grade, and algebra 2, which I failed the 2nd time around. If I can manage to pass both classes that will leave me just with the one failure...environmental science. I could pass to the 11th grade!

In the world history class I sat in the back with all the other stupid upper classmen. World history is a 9th grade course, but there were other sophomores, or wannabe sophomores like myself who flunked it the previous year. We all sat in the back; it was Rhonda Troy, sherry, and me. Rhonda was butt ugly with a huge set of tits, and Sherry was skinny, and ugly but a stone cold freak! Troy was just a cool guy. We would all laugh at how immature we thought the underclassmen were, we considered them babies.

All of us got kind of close. We would talk the entire class away! Sherry took a liking to me, and it was definitely one sided! I could hardly stand to look at her. She was about 5'10" tall, and weighed 93 pounds. This girl wore the biggest red frame glasses you could imagine. She made no secret of her desire to fuck the shit out of me!

Sherry would sit next to me in class, and whisper all kinds of kinky shit in my ear. I would close my eyes, and try to imagine it. Some of the crap she said sounded good, and my dick would get stiff as a board. Then I'd open my eyes, and instantly loose my erection when I saw her fucked up looking face!

I went all through summer school just enjoying the flirtatious relationship that we had I never acted on it believe me I Sherry was half way good looking I would have made it my business to fuck her repeatedly that summer.

When summer school ended so did the summer. At least one good thing happened, and that was I was going to 11th grade! I managed to pull off one of the biggest cloak, and dagger jobs of my life! I was glad to be back in my right grade and return to Lincoln with my head up high. I couldn't wait to step through those doors as a junior.

I was happy to be back in the familiar hallways of Abraham Lincoln. I was a junior with plenty of friends. I got a job, and had a wardrobe with all the fashionable clothes. I was ready to take this school year by storm! This was going to be my year I could feel it!

The familiar 88-bus ride was the same that first day as the 2 before it, loud and rowdy. I just knew I was the shit! I sat in the back, profiling with my black on black Adidas sweatsuit, and my fat gold rope with a big "RJ" medallion. To top off my outfit I was wearing my RUN-DMC leather blazer…I was the shit! I did the normal thing and stood out in front of the school with all my buddies to rate the incoming crop of girls it was another nice healthy crop I had to fuck one of them I just had too.

I was fully over Shante, and had a job at a business selling newspaper subscriptions over the phone. It may sound corny, but I was quite good at it. I have always been good at convincing people to do things that they didn't want to do, so I was a very good salesman. I was clearing about 200.00 a week! This was pretty good money for a kid with no bills. I made sure with that money that my wardrobe was tight. Judging by the looks I was getting from the ladies I did a good job. I strolled through the halls like a king! I was flirting with the ladies, people were stopping me saying hi all over the place. It really felt good! I didn't even care about my classes that year I knew I was going to ace them, especially after I had worked so hard to get to this point. I wasn't going to fuck up again.

Each day after school I would catch the bus and goto work. My new job was a couple of miles from the school the hours were 5 to 9 I got out of school at 2 I was cool with the manager so I would just hang out and talk with him until my shift began. This job was great it was my own personal pimping ground. Most of the people who worked there were young high school girls, and that was right up my alley. I was fucking just about every girl that came through the office. I was turning into a whore, and I loved it! I had a ton of gold jewelry, and the flyest gear out. That would attract the women like a magnet. All the girls would see how many sales I would get at work and ask, *"how did I do it?"* I would answer their question and use this as a way to start up a conversation, and that would be all she wrote! I was taking a different girl home almost nightly. I would fuck them, and send them home on the bus. I didn't have to worry about them hassling me at work, because people usually only lasted about 3 weeks at that job. By the time I closed the deal on fucking them, they got fired.

I was fucking and getting blown by plenty of hoes at work but I wasn't satisfied I still hadn't scored with any of the beauties at school and this is what I now set my sights on doing. My first victim was Sharon.

Sharon was a 10th grader who's locker was next to my Spanish class she caught my eye because she had a huge set of tits, her face was nothing to write home about, but those titties were too tempting a site to pass up. I started to flirt and talk with her whenever I would see her at her locker and I was coming or going to class eventually a friendship developed and now it was time for the kill no love just sex. I saw her one-day when I was on my way to history class. I pulled her to the side just as the bell rang. I should have been in class learning about the gold rush, but I had other things on my agenda. I told her I wanted to show her something, and I pulled her into the fire escape. We went behind the stairs; this was not a planned action this was all spur of the moment. As soon as we got back there I started to kiss her. The excitement level was tremendous because we were directly behind the stairs that people were using to goto class! Sharon was a good kisser, and I was on fire. I pulled her shirt open to have a look at those huge knockers. When I unleashed them from the massive harness she wore I was blown away…they were gorgeous! I started sucking on them like there was no tomorrow! I must have got caught up in the moment because before I knew it I knelt down, hiked her skirt up, and started to eat her pussy! She had a good-looking pussy! One of the best I have ever seen, I munched on her until I couldn't stand it anymore. I laid her on the floor, and stripped my clothes off. I was totally nude, except for a shirt. We were in the goddamn fire escape! Can you imagine if I had been caught? That fat ass Mr. Pushner would have loved that. Luckily, no one came back there. The moment was too exciting, and I could hold back no longer. I popped a full load deep inside her, and called it a day.

She wanted me to hang out with her afterwards, but I told her I had to get to class. I left her there under the stairs with a box full of jism. I spent the rest of the day thinking how incredible that experience was. Life was going along pretty good so I guess it was time for a monkey wrench.

I met Francis at my job, she was a 20-year-old college student we worked the same hours and became good friends but were total opposites. Francis was faithful, nerdy, gullible, and a virgin. I would joke about her all the time; to me she was a big goofball. Everytime I would come to work she was there. We became cool and started to goto lunch daily. After a while she became interested in me, without me even trying (that's my curse). I was kind of shocked, because she was older, not the oldest that I had been with (which was 38) but older. We began to date but she wasn't fucking so I definitely wasn't going to give up my hoes on the side. I would fuck girls in the daytime and take Francis out at night things were ok between us I was having a good wholesome time with Francis and letting my freak out with my other girls. I even managed to add another older girl to my stable a college girl began to sweat me too.

One night while Francis and I were going home after work she started to kiss me and grind on me she was really going at it right on the corner this virgin was on fire and practically trying to rape me! We went back to my house and luckily my mother wasn't home! Like that would have mattered! I fucked plenty of girls while she was fast asleep in her room and she never knew a thing.

Francis took a seat on the couch and I told her to chill for a minute because my brother was about to come downstairs and leave, but this girl couldn't; keep her hands off me she kept trying to stick her tongue down my throat and grab my dick. I was trying not to let my brother see her groping at my joint but this chick was all over me he left out the door and I could barely get out the words goodbye.

Once he was gone I took over. I led her straight up to my room undressed her and introduced her to womanhood. After we finally finished it was about 2 a.m. and I wanted to give her the customary Ok ill see you later" and boot her ass out the door. She only lived about 5 blocks away, so I did the gentlemanly thing and walked her home. On this 'long walk home' she kept looking at me, and finally asked me, *"do you want to be my man?"* I didn't really want to get with her like that so, I said *"NO!"*

I made up some bullshit story that I was hurt before, and didn't really want a relationship right now. I only said this so she wouldn't feel bad about being rejected. I figured that did it, I bid her farewell and went home. I hoped she wouldn't take it personal

I still wanted to be her friend but I didn't t want a relationship with her. I was having too good a time being free. I must have been drained from the previous night's activities because I didn't wake up until 4 p.m. the next day.

I slept through school when I finally woke up I had just enough time to hustle out and make it to work on time. On the way to work I thought about Francis I hoped that she wouldn't be disappointed about me turning her down.

When I walked into work all eyes were on me! They were all looking at me like I stole something it seems that big mouth Francis had told the whole office that I fucked her last night and refused to be in a relationship with her. Now this was big news considering

Everybody knew she was a virgin and they all wanted to be the one who fucked her. Now all the old bags were giving me the evil eye and she was heartbroken. I got sick and tired of seeing her mope around all evening so by the end of the night I gave in and she became my girlfriend.

The beginning....

Francis and I became inseparable. If we were not a work together, she was at my house. The only time I got a breather was when I made up some lie so I could get away and fuck girls. Oh yes, I still had a desire to fuck other girls. I found out about the number of something called the free party line.

The party line was a number that you could call, and once connected 13 other people all from Philly would be connected at one time. You could online, or exchange numbers. It was a wonderful way for me to meet new girls every girl was just the way I liked them...easy. On the line I was known as **"BIG DADDY"** and when I connected I would get straight to the point.

Who wants to get their pussy ate up? I would scream this as soon as I got on and plenty of ladies would reply back *"I DO, I DO!"*

I would tell them to take this number down and I would give them my number to call me that was the extent of my conversation online I would talk to these ladies for a couple of hours and then set up a meeting for the next day. I could usually convince them to dress up in a sexy outfit for me like a garter belt or thong when I was coming over and most of them would do it. I remember plenty of times I would show up at their door, and they would be waiting for me...naked.

These were girls I had never seen before, but I had their head so full with the crap I was telling them over the phone about how good I was going to make them feel when I got there. By the time I showed up they were hot for a fucking!

The party line was fun It provided me with sex atleast 3 times a week more if I really hustled, some of the girls showed me the freakier things like rubbing motion lotion on their pussies and working them with a dildo while I licked there tingling clit. I was having the time of my life no commitment just all sex and that's all I wanted I just moved on from one to the next there were too many ladies to fuck to be concerned with settling down with one.

Now my 11th year was done I passed everything with flying colors next year I was going to be a big senior I can't wait!

The first event of the summer was Francis lost her job selling newspapers. It seems there was this big scandal about someone making unauthorized long distance calls, and Francis got blamed for it. She got setup, she didn't make the calls and a few people in the office knew she didn't make the calls. These same people knew who did, and they never spoke up. The incident happened on a shift that she was running, so the company held her responsible and she was fired. It was a tough break for her, but atleast it allowed me to go back to the job I loved…office whore.

No sooner than she was out the door, I was back to my old tricks. I was handing out my phone number to the fresh new crop of female workers. I didn't waste anytime. Francis got a job at a local fast food place as a manager trainee. I was happy because it was closer to her house, and I got all the free burgers I could eat.

Another benefit was she worked longer hours, which gave me more time to go on fuck expeditions.

Francis lived with her aunt. Her aunt was mean, and crazy. The house they lived in was a pigsty! I don't know how anyone could stand living there. The living room was cluttered with all kinds of old junk. Newspapers were scattered all over the floor, and junk furniture was everywhere! Her aunt had a penchant for trash picking, and she would pick up all kinds of worthless crap. She would pick up junk and just lay it in her house. The stuff she would pick up served no purpose. She just collected crap to collect it. If an old coffeepot was on the ground she would pick it up take it home, and sit it on the floor. There the junk would stay, what the heck is that? One time she found an old bus map in the trash at a bus depot you know the kind that showed all the stops on a bus route it was all covered with paint and was illegible she took it home and hung it on the wall who needs that? She was a strange one, and god forbid you try to clean things up. She would threaten to kick you out if you even tried to pick up a broom! The refrigerator was a nightmare! If you even thought you were thirsty you'd better think again. The fridge was like a garbage can. There were open cans of greens just sitting in there uncovered. Year old hot dogs, and pickles from when Francis was a kid! I see why Francis always ate out; can you imagine having stuff in your refrigerator for so long? It was apparent that shopping was something that wasn't done in this household. I was sick everytime I stepped into this cesspool of a house. I won't even bring up the bathroom, to top it all off the woman had about 10 cats. These weren't normal house cats, these were rough alley cats that she just found roaming in her backyard, and decided to let them crash at her house...indefinitely. Francis told me stories about the basement. The basement was like Vietnam. A big hole was in the window, so in addition to all the junk that was in there all the animals used the basement as their own private speakeasy. It was common to hear all kinds of noises coming from behind the basement door I was no coward but you couldn't pay me to step foot down those stairs the light didn't even work if I went down there it would be like a one way trip to hell.

One day Francis was looking on her aunt's dresser for a safety pin and she came across her tax refund check and it was already opened. She took the check out of the open envelope, and looked at the postmark. It had been there for 4 weeks. She confronted her aunt about it immediately. Her aunt told her that she wanted half the money, and since it was her house she can keep the mail for however long she wants to, and distributes it when she feels like it. They got into a huge argument, which ended up with Francis having to leave the house. I came to the rescue when this happened.

Since Francis was cool with my entire family, I sort of greased the way for her to come and live with us.

UH OH! I just made the biggest mistake of my life! I realized it a few weeks after she moved in don't get me wrong for a while it was great! A constant convenient supply of sex and an in home maid it was wonderful until my doggish ways came out.

At work there was this girl with the biggest set of tits I had ever seen I wanted her **BAD!** I started to kick it to her and after a few days I got her to agree to come over my house now there was only one problem…Francis.

I told the girl to come over Saturday after we got off work. Francis would be at work by the time I got home, and everybody else would be upstairs. I would have a window of about 3 hours to close the deal with this girl, and get her the hell out of the house before Francis got home. We got to my house, and went directly to the basement .she wasn't a virgin, and neither was I. For some reason she intimidated me. Maybe it was because I was so focused on those giant breasts that I couldn't think about anything else, but I really wanted to give it to her good. I put a blanket down on the floor, and started to kiss her. My hands roamed all over her gorgeous body. Then it happened…I removed her shirt. She had on a giant harness. It was like a bulletproof vest. It went from the top of her lovely tits to her waist! It was a giant industrial sized bra! I had to use both hands to release the straight jacket that held in her marvelous chest. When I finally undid the last buckle, let those melons loose from imprisonment I couldn't believe my eyes. The titties were huge! I marveled at them for a moment then I went to work on them like a starving newborn baby. I sucked like a madman. I even put her in different positions just to suck those beauties. After an eternity of big tit sucking, I decided it was time I knocked that ass off! I was rock hard, so I made the move to unbutton her pants…big mistake!

When I pulled her pants down I was hit with the worst stench I have ever smelled in my life this girls pussy smelled like a cesspool I started o look around because I thought that perhaps the sewage pipe had burst but that wasn't it.

It was her! **This girls snatch smelled like a dead man!** Now with a box that stinky you would think she would have been a little self conscious, but she wasn't. This filthy pig had the nerve to spread her stinking ass legs as wide as she could and say, *"Aren't you going to eat me?"* I almost gagged this bitch wanted me to put my tongue in the garbage heap she called a pussy? **She must be crazy!** I thought I was going to barf. I just ignored her request, and said to myself I came this far I'm just going to fuck her anyway. As I went to mount her I noticed that my dick was as limp as can be. I was disgusted by her vaginal wastebasket, and I could no longer get it up. I tried everything. I even took my dick, and rubbed it up against her sour snatch but nothing. My dick had gone into hibernation. After a few attempts she got frustrated, I got nauseous so we stopped. I was glad I atleast got to see those beautiful melons, but I could have done without that landfill she called a pussy. I hustled her out the door and went to disinfect myself…. What a waste!

Shortly after the episode with this girl she went the way of my other at work conquests she got fired it was now time for a fresh crop.

As the days went on things started to deteriorate between Francis and me. I was tired of her constantly being up under me, and plus I wanted to fuck everything that moved. Of all the extra fucking I did she never actually busted me with any of the hoes I was banging. I had a lot of close calls, but I was never caught.

Things finally got to the breaking point and by the end of the summer Francis moved out! **HOORAY!** I was finally free she was gone I could now do whatever I wanted to!

12th grade was here finally after a summer filled with sex (which seemed to consume my whole life) I was finally a senior and would be graduating I would be the first real high school graduate of all my siblings I was very excited about the coming year…

What a disappointment! Senior year wasn't all it's cracked up to be. I thought it was pretty unexciting. Other than getting much respect because I was a senior, and flaunting my *'I'm going to be done with school soon'* status infront of the underclassmen, I really didn't have too many exciting things happen. One was a constant…and that was sex.

I was like a sex machine. In school I was banging them in the fire escape, or at their home. I also got into whacking off to porn.

I would get porn flicks from the little record shops downtown, and rush home to see them. We only had 1 VCR in the living room, so I had to wait until everybody was upstairs. Then I would creep down into the living room, and slip in the tape. I had to keep the volume low, but it was just loud enough so I could hear the moans. I would sit infront of the TV with my pants down around my ankles. I had a hand full of lotion, and I would pump my dick like there was no tomorrow! I would watch the scenes, and see how long I could hold out before I shot gobs of cum all over the floor. Sometimes I would reach the screen! I was doing this about twice a day! I would rub the cum I shot on the floor into the carpet. After a while the carpet became stained with noticeable white splotches. Everytime I walked by I would wonder if anybody else noticed. If they didn't know then what they were they know now.

Graduation day was the most boring day of my life I kept nodding off during the program I had been up for the entire night before fucking I had a marathon session I went not once not twice but three times a personal best! I couldn't wait for the never ending speeches and award presentations to be over when the borefest finally ended I rejoiced got my diploma and got the fuck out of there! We went to one of my favorite restaurants at the time…Pat's steaks (what do you expect I was a kid). We all had a nice big cheese steak. Not everybody would have picked that place for a celebration dinner, but to me pat's was 5 star quisine.

After graduation the summer came, and went. Adult life is here, and I'm on my way to college. That means more years of school, and books. I have definitely learned from high school, no more playing around for me. My mother never found out about me getting left down. I didn't tell her until I was about 25. I felt that was a safe age for us to have a laugh about it. When I think back these were some of the best times of my life! I only hope that one day I learn from all of the lessons I got in these life experiences, and do the right thing.

About the Author

RJ Davenport was born in 1971, and raised in the ghettos of Philadelphia. Product of a single parent home, he survived and overcame the same adversities that are constantly used as an excuse today.

He has evolved into a successful Computer Consultant and published Author. Choosing not succumb to intoxicating draw of the fast life. Following the rule of not waiting for anyone to give him anything, he struggled and fought his way out of poverty to achieve his goals.

RJ is a good, and more importantly a **POSITIVE**, role model for the black youth of America.